Praise for *The Answers Are Within You & Amber Rae*

"*The Answers Are Within You* is a book for everyone—creatives looking to explore their art, students just starting to discern their life dreams, and entrepreneurs gathering the confidence to take their next big leap. Amber Rae gives us the courage to trust our own intuition and step into the world with wonder and joy."

—**Gay Hendricks, Ph.D.**, author of *The Big Leap* and *The Genius Zone*

"*The Answers Are Within You* is a phenomenal visual guide that can help anyone who is ready to grow deeply. Amber Rae reconnects you to a clear perspective so you can reclaim your power and allow the best version of yourself to come forward."

—**Yung Pueblo**, *New York Times* bestselling author of *Clarity & Connection*

"I love this book! It's like having a fantastic therapist or coach give you brilliant advice wrapped up in candy! Every time I looked at one of Amber Rae's pieces of word art, the wisdom just jumped off the page, bypassed my brain, and landed in my bloodstream. It makes total sense to me that inspired wisdom needs to truly be delivered like this . . . in an inspired way."

—**Tama Kieves**, *USA Today*–featured visionary career coach and bestselling author of *A Year Without Fear* and *Thriving Through Uncertainty*

"*The Answers Are Within You* offers keen insights that cut to the core of the human condition. The agony and the bliss. The responsibility and the awe. The sense of wonder. This book helps lead the way with courage."

—**Jason Silva**, Emmy-nominated TV personality, filmmaker, and storyteller

"*The Answers Are Within You* is a twofold gift—it's both a beautiful book with art that captures your heart and deeply wise—with powerful insight that reaches the center of our emotional lives."

—**Tina Roth Eisenberg**, founder of CreativeMornings

"A beautiful collection for anyone looking to unearth their inner magic and gain emotional clarity."

—**Alexandra Elle**, author of *After the Rain*

"What Brené Brown is to vulnerability, Amber Rae is to wonder."

—**mindbodygreen**

"Amber doesn't just bring wisdom and insights—she brings meaning."

—***Entrepreneur***

The
ANSWERS
are WITHIN
you

Also by Amber Rae

Choose Wonder over Worry

The
ANSWERS
are WITHIN
you

108 Keys to Unlock Your
Mind, Body & Soul

Amber Rae

ST. MARTIN'S
ESSENTIALS
NEW YORK

First published in the United States by St. Martin's Essentials, an imprint of St. Martin's Publishing Group

THE ANSWERS ARE WITHIN YOU. Copyright © 2021 by Amber Rae. All rights reserved. Printed in China. For information, address St. Martin's Publishing Group, 120 Broadway, New York, NY 10271.

www.stmartins.com

Illustrations created by Amber Rae and Maddie Nieman

The Library of Congress Cataloging-in-Publication Data is available upon request.

ISBN 978-1-250-80935-3 (paper over board)
ISBN 978-1-250-80936-0 (ebook)

Our books may be purchased in bulk for promotional, educational, or business use. Please contact your local bookseller or the Macmillan Corporate and Premium Sales Department at 1-800-221-7945, extension 5442, or by email at MacmillanSpecialMarkets@macmillan.com.

First Edition: 2022

10 9 8 7 6 5 4 3 2 1

For you, who's on the journey
of looking within

Contents

Introduction

I've been writing about self-discovery, emotional wellness, creativity, and following one's calling for over a decade now. A few years ago, I decided to try an experiment. I wondered:

How might I take the concepts I write about—self-trust, how to feel your feelings, being kind to your mind, setting boundaries, having hard conversations, unlocking creativity, sourcing wisdom from within, and so on—and express them visually?

My intent was to take ideas that felt intangible and complex and make them simple and digestible. I turned to Instagram to share these frameworks, prompts, and illustrations with my community—and what happened next astounded me.

The artwork and ideas spread further than I ever could have imagined. Hundreds of millions of people from all corners of the globe shared my work and how they used them—in classrooms and therapy sessions; to spark conversations at dinner tables and with loved ones; as a companion for self-reflection and journaling; as potent reminders inside work spaces and at home.

Messages poured in from all ages and walks of life. Fathers told me stories of learning to better communicate with their daughters. Women wrote to me about being able to finally get quiet and hear their intuition. College students shared that they were able to navigate anxiety with more ease. Aspiring creators were *finally* taking the leap. Couples were creating connection through conflict. Teachers were helping their students check in with their feelings before math or science. Actors were finding their ways through overwhelm and burnout. Entrepreneurs were learning to find joy in the journey.

I heard from every kind of human about every area of their lives. At the core of each story, the epiphany I heard is this:

When I get quiet and create the space to really hear myself, I know what to do to feel joyful, whole, and complete. The answers are within *me*.

Yes, love—the answers are within *you*.

We live in a world that teaches us to look **outside** to experts, to teachers, and even to Google for answers to our most important questions. It is so ingrained in many of us that we may not even realize how often we outsource our own knowing. The reason we seek the answers outside is because we don't know how to access them from within.

I created this book to give you the clarity and courage to listen to and trust yourself— through beautiful, bite-size sparks of wisdom. It compiles the illustrations that have spread far and wide, with many others that are brand-new.

You can think of this book as your treasure chest.

Each page is a key that helps you unlock the treasures and truths that live within. The pages won't tell you what to do (only you know that); instead, they'll show you what to ask and how to listen—so you can access your own answers.

I designed this book for you to read however you'd like—page by page, or in random order. There's a journey to the pages, but they're also meant to stand alone. You can use it like an "oracle book" (my personal favorite) by closing your eyes, bringing to mind a question, and opening the book to a "random" page—to see what message is meant for you. Or you can use the table of contents to find a topic that feels timely. Let this book show up for you how you'd most enjoy. No rules.

As you explore these pages, my greatest hope is that they help you connect more deeply with yourself and those you love—so that you may live your one life in the way that feels most authentic and true. I hope each prompt reminds you that the answers you seek live within you—today and always.

xo
Amber Rae

February 11, 2021

2:22 p.m.

Baja California

P.S. Sharing any of these pages on social media?

Tag **@heyamberrae** #answersarewithin so we can all find each other.

Them

Me

↑

↑

Where I looked
for approval

Where I
found it

Approval Comes from Within

If there's one thing I'd tell my younger self, it's this:

Approval isn't out there; it's found *in you.*

When you place your lovability and self-worth in the hands of another, that's self-betrayal, my love. When you look to others for validation that you're "good enough" or doing it "right," you'll only gain distance from your true self.

Look inside and listen to your own knowing.

You're the only one who's present for every moment of your life. When you make choices based on what's right and true for you, rather than what others expect, you'll create a life that's authentic to you. Others' opinions will begin to fade into the background as you honor and trust what brings *you* meaning and joy.

When the noise of the outside world gets too loud—which it inevitably will—remember to pause, get still, and ask yourself:

What feels right and true *for me*?

Let that question simmer until an answer arises from within. Then go live it.

THE FEAR
It's already been done.
THE TRUTH
It hasn't been done by you.

Commit to Your Gifts

I was talking with a novelist about a book she's been thinking about for ten years. *(Ten years!)* When I asked her where she's at with it and when I can read it, she said, "Oh, I don't know. So many people write novels. I don't know if it's worth doing. It's already been done, anyway."

Of all the fears I hear when people tell me about their callings and dreams, "It's already been done" is one that really stings my heart.

Because, yes, of course, millions of books and films and artworks and innovations exist in the world. But want to know what's also true?

None of them have been made *by you*.

When you translate your life experiences, worldviews, and emotions into creating something—something that reflects your curiosities and life story—that's what makes your work authentic, original, and unique.

So if you've ever stalled because "it's already been done"—remember this, love:

Maybe it's been done. But it hasn't been done *by you*.

Committing to your gifts will bring so much magic, joy, surprise, and delight into your life—that is, if you say "yes" to them. Consider this an invitation to take one tiny step toward the thing that calls at you today.

Find Clarity Through Action

A pharmacist reached out to me about getting in touch with her inner artist. As she shared her curiosities and dreams with me, each one was followed by a series of "what-ifs":

What if I don't like doing that? What if I'm not good at it? What if it doesn't work out? What if it turns out different than what I think? What if I waste my time?

What if . . . What if . . . What if . . .

Our conversation reminded me of the times I was on the verge of leaping into a new direction but was stuck in that "in-between" stage of trying to figure *everything* out before taking the first step.

Whether it was leaving the world of tech to pursue a more creative path, choosing to go "all in" on a relationship, or making a meaningful shift in my business—I once believed that I needed to have the "perfect plan" to get started.

Here's the truth, though: there are no perfect plans. Clarity comes through taking action.

CLARITY COMES STEP BY STEP

We won't know what works or doesn't work and what feels right or doesn't feel right until we see, feel, and experience it. It's then, and only then, that we'll have the wisdom and insight to adjust and evolve—and make more informed choices moving forward.

What have you been waiting to pursue until you have the perfect plan? What might instead be your very next small step?

Remember: clarity comes through taking action. Step by step by step.

Be

OPEN

to failure

Be Open to Failure

"But what if I fail?"

You know that anxious feeling—that you may mess up or fall short. Where does it come from?

For many of us, we grow up hearing that we learn best by doing. Yet when we do get things wrong—which we all inevitably do—we're often criticized, shamed, and ridiculed. It's no wonder that we fear failure, turn up the volume on perfectionism, and hold back our gifts.

What's helped me move beyond the fear of failure is by thinking of my life and work as an experiment. This gives me the space to try things on, see how they feel, and make adjustments as I go. I'm not locked into a pressure-filled container of needing to get it "right"; I'm allowing myself to learn, make mistakes, and fail forward.

So the next time you worry: But what if I fail? I invite you to ask a different question: Am I *willing* to fail? And if so: How will I respond when I do?

There are always one of two ways to respond to failure:

1. As a reflection of your self-worth (not very helpful)

2. As a *very* normal part of the process (*much* more helpful)

Remember: by discovering what *doesn't* work, you're one step closer to what *will*. So *celebrate* the missteps just as much as the milestones.

It's time to be brave. In what small way will you open up to failure today?

Don't Feed Your Fears

I'd like to have a heart-to-heart with whoever started the rumor that you have to be fearless to pursue your dreams. Fearlessness is a myth. A block. An unnecessary and unattainable goal.

Here's why: fear is not your enemy. Fear is not a part of you that you need to go to war with and try to "overcome." Fear has been wired into your system for millions of years as a mechanism to keep you safe. The truth is, you *need* your fear.

Thanks to fear, we're not getting in cars with strangers and we're not jumping off the sides of mountains to see if we can make the landing. Fear tells us, "Bad idea. Very dangerous. Do not proceed." That kind of fear is helpful.

There are times, however, when fear can be *less* helpful. Like when it comes to acting on what's meaningful and important and true, otherwise known to fear as unknown and potentially life-threatening.

When I was writing my first book, for example, fear was very set on the idea that my vulnerable style of writing was going to leave me crucified. Fear would shout, "DO NOT DARE WRITE THE NEXT SENTENCE. You may die. Judgment is impending."

Rather than see fear as a signal that something was wrong, that I wasn't doing it right, or that I needed to halt all activity and proceed with caution, I learned to see fear as a directive. Scared means "I care."

What if What if What if What
What What if What if What if if
if what if What if What if
What if What if What if What
What What if What if What if if
if what if What if What if

What is

Focus on What Is, Not What If

Our minds can get so caught up in imaginary what-if futures that we lose touch with what *is*.

> How am I feeling in my body?
>
> What am I noticing that I need?
>
> Where is my curiosity pointing me?
>
> What is energizing me most right now?
>
> What small steps will I take today?

Rather than exhaust our energy in a future we can't control or a past we can't change, we can center instead on the truth of what's right here, right now—and then take empowered steps toward our desired future.

What *if* is a trap. What *is* is a compass—pointing you in the direction of your most meaningful next step.

WHY AM I DOING THIS?

for LOVE **or** from LOVE

for JOY **or** from JOY

for MORE **or** from MORE

for POWER **or** from POWER

Do Things from Love

Why do you do what you do?

My friend Brad Montague, an author, illustrator, and the creator of the web series *Kid President*, once shared with me, "Sometimes we do things *for* love or *for* satisfaction when we could be doing things *from* love or *from* a deep satisfaction."

His wisdom got me thinking . . .

Am I operating *for* joy or *from* deep joy?

Am I doing this *for more* (e.g., impact, reach) or *from more* (e.g., self-worth and knowing I'm already enough)?

Am I being motivated *for power* or am I acting *from power*?

Whenever I feel stuck or disconnected from what I'm doing, I'll often find that my motivation is out of alignment with what I truly value. When I recalibrate and reorient my focus, I naturally return to a state of internal alignment and flow.

What is motivating you—the *for* or the *from*?

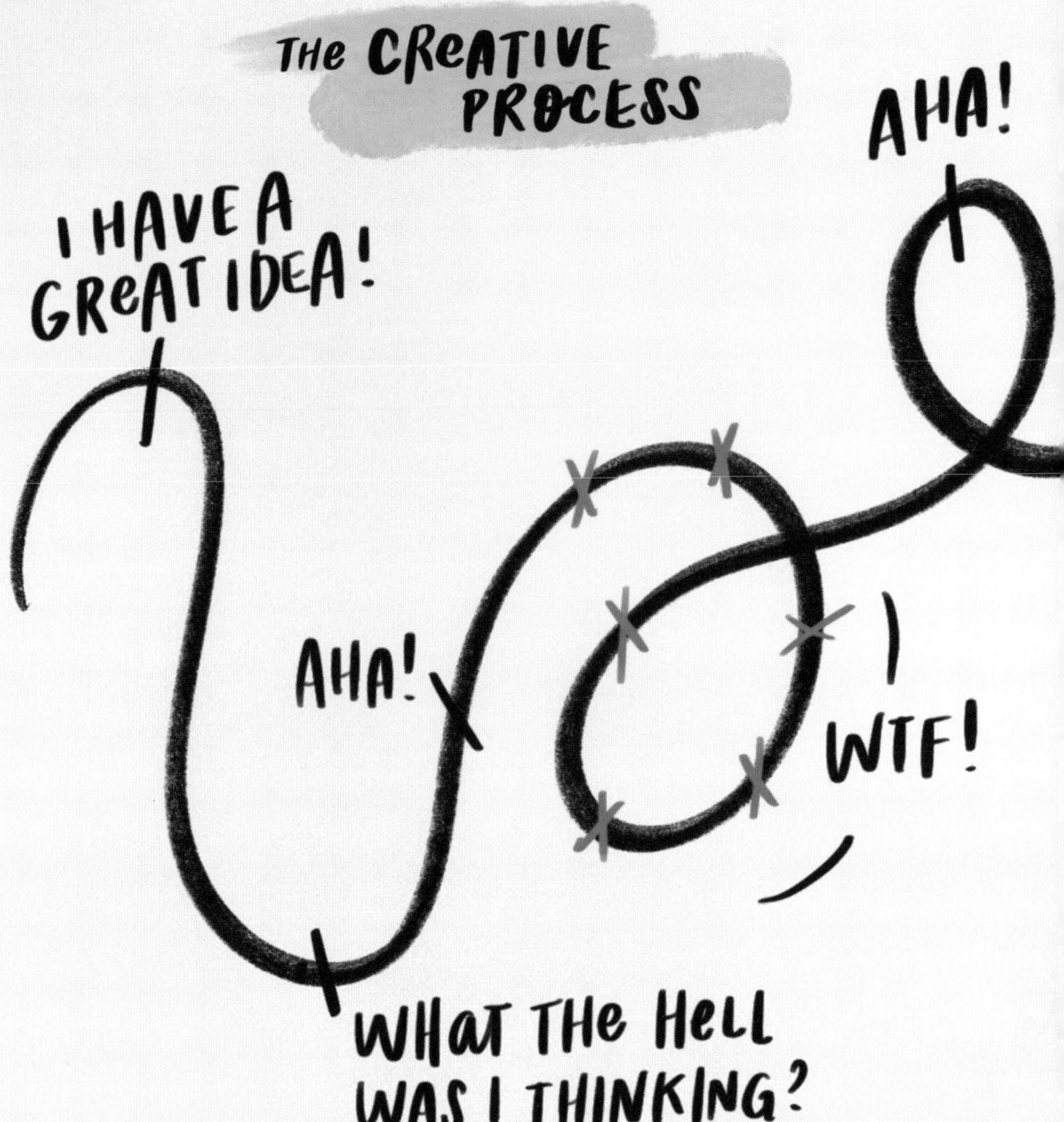
THE CREATIVE PROCESS
I HAVE A GREAT IDEA!
AHA!
AHA!
WTF!
WHAT THE HELL WAS I THINKING?

IT ALL MAKES SENSE NOW!

Ride the Creative Zigzag

Maybe you can relate to this ebb-and-flow journey?

If the thing you're working on matters to your heart, I have one piece of wisdom to share: keep going.

Sure, take a break if you're tired. Ask for help if you need support. Go on a walk, journal your anxiety out, enjoy a laugh with friends, or have a good cry.

But please: do not give up. Your fears may tell you otherwise. Your mind may spin stories. The WTF stage may go on longer than you'd like.

Here's what I know to also be true: those OMG, WTF, get-me-out-of-here moments tend to occur when we're on the brink of a big breakthrough.

So keep going. Your resilience is expanding with every step.

You are
not the
voice inside
your head

You Are Not the Voice Inside Your Head

One of the bigger, life-changing aha! moments I experienced was when I realized that I am not the voice inside my head.

It was liberating to discover that so much of my suffering and anguish was due to the fact that I was listening to, and believing, the constant stream of critical chatter and fearful thoughts that I heard ricocheting around my mind.

"This is good. . . . This is bad. . . . I don't like that. . . . I should have said that. . . . Is something wrong with me? . . . Did I do something wrong? . . . Is my life a mess? . . . Will I end up forever alone and unloved?"

In a matter of minutes, I was capable of creating a whole world of drama inside my mind and it wasn't even 10 a.m. on a Tuesday.

The breakthrough happened when I recognized two things:

1. Alongside the chatter is the part of me **witnessing and observing the chatter.** With that awareness comes a choice on how to engage and respond.

2. It's helpful to engage with a healthy dose of curiosity and humor. That's how "Will I end up forever alone and unloved?" can become "Girl, please. It's 10 a.m. and you're *hangry*. Let's eat before we contemplate life's worst-case scenarios."

So the next time you catch yourself crafting a Netflix-worthy drama series in your mind, consider this a reminder to pause, notice the part of you that's pausing (the Observer), and remind yourself:

I am not the voice inside my head.

Right move — Right move — Right move

Right move — Right move — Right move

Right move — Right move

Make the Next Right Move

A few years ago, I sat in the front row at the United Nations to hear Oprah speak. (I actually took her seat by accident—but that's a different story.)

She opened up to us, sharing that when she decided to start OWN after more than twenty-five years of *The Oprah Winfrey Show* being a number-one success, she never anticipated the challenges she'd run into.

When she found herself flustered, stressed, off track, and on the edge of a breakdown—listening to what she calls "little person mind"—she couldn't hear herself clearly. The way she moved through the fog was to get still and ask herself one simple question:

What is the next right move?

She asked and acted on that question until she moved out from the darkness and back into the light.

Bring to mind a situation that's creating stress or tension in your life right now, and ask yourself:

What is the next right move?

Then act. One small move at a time.

Feel your Feelings. Don't become them.

Feel Your Feelings, Don't Become Them

Let's talk about the difference between *feeling* your emotions and *becoming* them.

Feeling an emotion looks like noticing a sensation, acknowledging its presence, and allowing it to move through your system. It's remembering that you are not the feeling or the thoughts, but rather the vessel through which the sensation can come and go.

Becoming an emotion, on the other hand, is when you allow the emotion to take over. It looks like jumping into stories about situations (like "This is bad," "Something is wrong with me," or "I shouldn't be feeling this") and spiraling into thinking the future will be worse than the present.

If we're not careful, we can take on the emotion itself, quite literally becoming sadness or anger or fear—sometimes for days or weeks—when we allow the emotion to overstay its welcome.

On the other hand, when we allow ourselves to feel an emotion without attaching too much meaning to it, we give the feeling a chance to move through us, teach us, transform us, and then leave us.

Your emotions are like weather patterns: they come and they go. Sometimes they impact how we think and behave in the moment, but every emotion eventually clears, and we're left with a fresh page once again.

Remember: you are the sky, not the weather. This too shall pass.

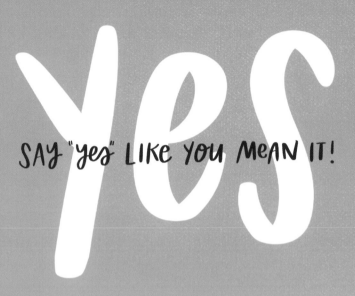

SAY "yes" LIKE YOU MEAN IT!

Say "Yes" Like You Mean It

You know those moments when you say "yes" when you don't actually mean it?

Here's why you might say "yes" when what you *really* mean is "no," "not now," or, "not sure yet":

1. You're afraid of disappointing someone.

2. You don't want to be perceived as unlikeable, uncaring, or unhelpful.

3. You're worried the other person will feel rejected or hurt.

4. You fear you'll miss out on something if you don't say "yes."

5. You genuinely aren't sure and feel like you have to have an answer right now.

For these reasons and more, you might say "yes" to avoid conflict and seem "easygoing." You might even find yourself adjusting who you are and what you stand for in an attempt to fit in and be liked.

As a recovering people pleaser, here's the hard-earned truth: when you need to adjust yourself (read: *abandon* and *betray* yourself) to fit what someone else wants, it can't last or work. It very well *may* last for weeks or months or years, but my guess is that 1. it won't work very well, and 2. there will come a day when you realize that you can no longer fake your life.

My loving reminder to you is this: **you always have a choice**. You can live a life of comfortable lies and playing pretend, or you can say "yes" to life like you mean it.

Saying "yes" like you mean it means saying "no" to that which is incongruent with who you are, what you value, and what you stand for.

Saying "yes" like you mean it means that when opportunities arise, you take a moment to get *really* still and quiet, to check in with the core of your being and ask, "Is this right and true for me? Like, for real, for *real* . . . is this right and true *for me*?"

Saying "yes" like you mean it may not feel like the easy path, but I promise you this: it is the most worthwhile one. Because living as you are, and not as who you were conditioned or applauded to be, is one of the most courageous things you can do in your lifetime.

My sense is that you're reading these words now because you've chosen to live a life that is more strongly led by courage than comfort—so if there's an area of your life where you feel like you're playing pretend, I leave with you with this:

It's time to say "yes" like you mean it.

WHEN to STOP GIVING SOMETHING YOUR ATTENTION

1. You stopped learning

2. It's not useful

3. It takes a mental or emotional toll

4. You no longer enjoy it

Choose Where Your Energy Goes

Let this be a permission slip: just because you start something, doesn't mean you have to finish it. Commitment and follow-through are important qualities, though so too is remaining flexible when your priorities and passions shift.

I once believed that if I didn't follow through on every single thing I set out to do, it meant I was a "flaky person." This led me to stay in projects that were taking a mental and emotional toll, and it had me orient my energy on relationships and activities that drained me.

I hope you find comfort in this truth: your time and attention are two of your most valuable resources, and you get to choose where your energy goes. When a commitment no longer brings you joy, creates meaning in your life, or represents who and what you stand for, that's a clue to check in with yourself and reevaluate. Maybe it's time to adjust your role, or perhaps it's time to let go.

Take a moment to consider where you've been directing your energy and attention lately. Are there any activities that are draining you? Beliefs that are limiting you? Projects you've outgrown? Or relationships that are stifling you?

Remember: you get to choose where your energy goes.

PERMISSION SLIP
I WANT TO
DO MORE ___
PERMISSION SLIP
I WANT TO
DO LESS ___

Name Your Needs

Take a moment to tune in to your body.

Take a deep breath, wiggle your shoulders, unclench your jaw, close your eyes, and then tune in.

How do you feel? Do you notice any tension or tightness? Do you notice any excitement or ease? Take thirty seconds to observe the sensations in your body without judgment.

Now that you've tuned in, get curious: What do you need most right now?

Maybe it's more rest, more play, more truth-telling, or more focus.

Maybe it's less self-judgment, less control, less rushing, or fewer distractions.

Whatever it is for you—take a moment to declare your desires and name your needs. Know that whatever you need is the most productive thing you can do for yourself, even if it might feel counterproductive.

Write yourself two permission slips—and then go live what you've written.

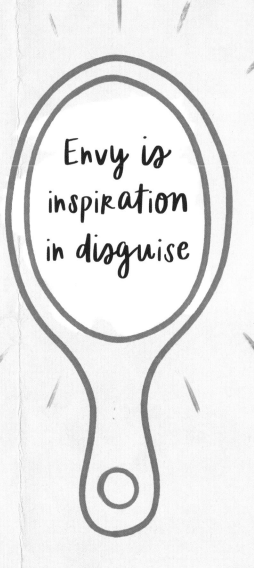

Find Inspiration in Envy

It's natural to flip through social media and experience thoughts like, "I'm so behind." "They're better off than me." "Why not me?" We may judge who we feel envious of or beat ourselves up for feeling less than—falling into a trap of comparison.

But guess what? There's another, more empowering way to respond: we can see envy as a mirror that's reflecting our own curiosities, longings, and desires.

Let's say you feel envy every time you see someone publish a book, for example. That could be a clue that you yearn to write your own book, too. Or if you notice envy when you're around a couple that's madly in love, that too could be an invitation to make dating a priority—and not to settle.

When we view our envy toward others not as proof of our own shortcomings but, instead, as a shining example of what we want to grow into, that's how envy becomes our muse.

The next time you notice envy, find the inspiration in it by wondering:

What is it that I'm envious about here?

Why am I envious?

What does that tell me about my own true desires?

And what's my next step?

LISTEN WITH YOUR WHOLE BODY

A dear friend texted me, asking, "How do you make aligned decisions?"

"I listen to my body," I replied. "My *whole* body."

I learned this through the many times I did *not* listen to my body, and instead, listened to my mind. This is when my mind says, "This is a smart decision and makes sense for you," but my shoulders are tightening, my jaw is clenching, my fists are forming, and my chest is caving inward. If I ignore the signals of my body and rationalize the decision, I begin to walk a path that's not meant for me.

(Friendly reminder: if you've recently made a decision that's not aligned, or you're now walking a path that's not meant for you, consider this permission to change your mind and shift course. Celebrate, rather than criticize, your newfound awareness.)

Having a *lot* of experience with shifting course led me to discover a life-changing perspective from psychologist Martha Beck: to let my body navigate and my mind implement. This is the practice of trusting my body to be the compass that makes wise decisions. When considering a decision or direction, I'll listen for my body to say a wholehearted "yes," which feels like my shoulders relaxing, my chest opening, and an overall state of energy, eagerness, and surrender. There might be nervousness there, too—or "nerve-citement"—but even so, that sensation is connected to the anticipation of what could be and the recognition that when following what's true, there is always the possibility of loss or heartbreak. Once I can feel that my body is signaling "yes," that's when I invite my mind in to do what it does best: dream, strategize, plan, and implement.

Listening to and acting on the wisdom of your body is a practice that may require many steps forward and back. As you go about your day today, let it be a chance to tune in. Notice when a song gives you goose bumps, when the words from a friend create ease in your shoulders, or when something you hear causes your chest to tighten and cave in. Notice what feels light and what feels heavy, what feels expansive and what feels constricting. Notice when your feet tap to music or your hands move when you speak. Notice what draws you in and what pulls you away.

As you notice, you'll tap into the force field of wisdom that is your body, and bring awareness to its potent clues. You'll learn to see where your curiosity and intuition are pointing you and when your body is saying "not for me" or "this way, please."

Let today be a day to notice, listen, and let your whole body lead.

5 THINGS
TO TELL
YOURSELF
WHEN YOU'RE
FEELING
ALL THE FEELS

I'm safe

It's okay to feel this way

This feeling is temporary

I will get through this

Right now, I need _____

OUR
FEELINGS AREN'T
THE PROBLEM.
IT'S OUR
RELATIONSHIP
TO THEM.

Embrace Your Emotions

Many of us learn when growing up that emotions are "good" or "bad." We should feel the "positive" ones and shut down the "negative" ones. Not only is this misguided, it's harmful.

When we push our emotions away, act like everything is okay when it's not, and put on a happy face, it prevents us from living authentically and finding wisdom in our emotions. Emotions aren't "good" or "bad"—they're neutral messengers that invite us to meet our needs and move toward wholeness.

As we learn to view emotions as evidence of our humanity and not of our brokenness, we open a doorway to the part of us that longs for our attention. That's how emotions become allies on our path.

Anger, for instance, instructs us to act on our boundaries and limits.

Sadness points to a part of us that wants attention and care.

Joy helps pave the way to our purpose and freedom.

Compassion inspires us to meet others (and ourselves) exactly as we are.

So the next time a challenging emotion greets you, remember: your feeling isn't the problem, it's how you relate to it. Instead of wronging or shaming yourself, welcome the emotion with curiosity as if you were meeting an honored guest.

You might try saying, "Oh hello, dear emotion! Why are you here? What is it that you want me to know?" Then lean in and listen like you're having tea with your wisest new best friend.

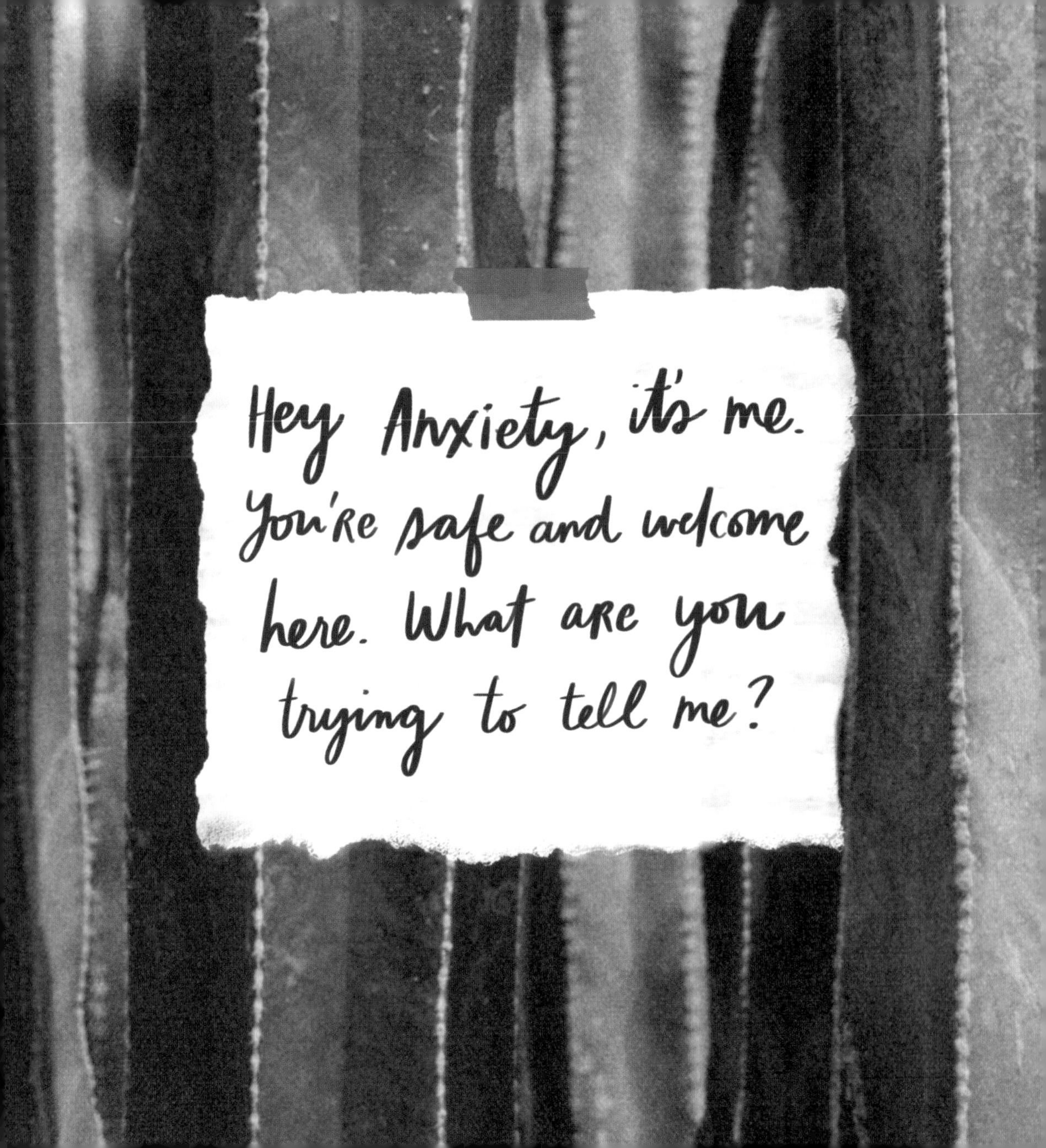
Hey Anxiety, it's me.
You're safe and welcome
here. What are you
trying to tell me?

Mine for Inner Treasure

Journaling is a tool I use to give challenging emotions a chance to speak and feel heard through the page. It helps me process what I'm going through, and it feels like I'm handing the emotion a microphone so it can communicate its needs with me. I often won't know what the emotion has to say until I start writing, and the insights that come through will often surprise me.

Here's how the practice works:

Start by picking an emotion that's been present for you lately. Maybe you've noticed yourself feeling anxious, bored, lonely, sad, scared, tired, or overwhelmed. Whatever it is, know that it's okay to feel that way. Your emotions are wise messengers, nudging for your attention.

TRY THIS

With that in mind, at the top of your journal page, write:

Hey [the emotion of your choice], *it's me,* [your name]. *You're safe and welcome here. I'm here to listen. What are you trying to tell me? How are you trying to help me?*

Next, free-flow write, as if the emotion were speaking to you, until it feels seen and heard. I find it helpful to set a timer for ten minutes and to write whatever comes up first, even if that's "I don't know what I'm trying to tell you." This creates the space to move past the inner editor so that we can reach the deeper wisdom.

Over time, as you practice journaling with your feelings, you'll find it easier to unearth treasure in your innermost terrain.

MAKE MORE MISTAKES

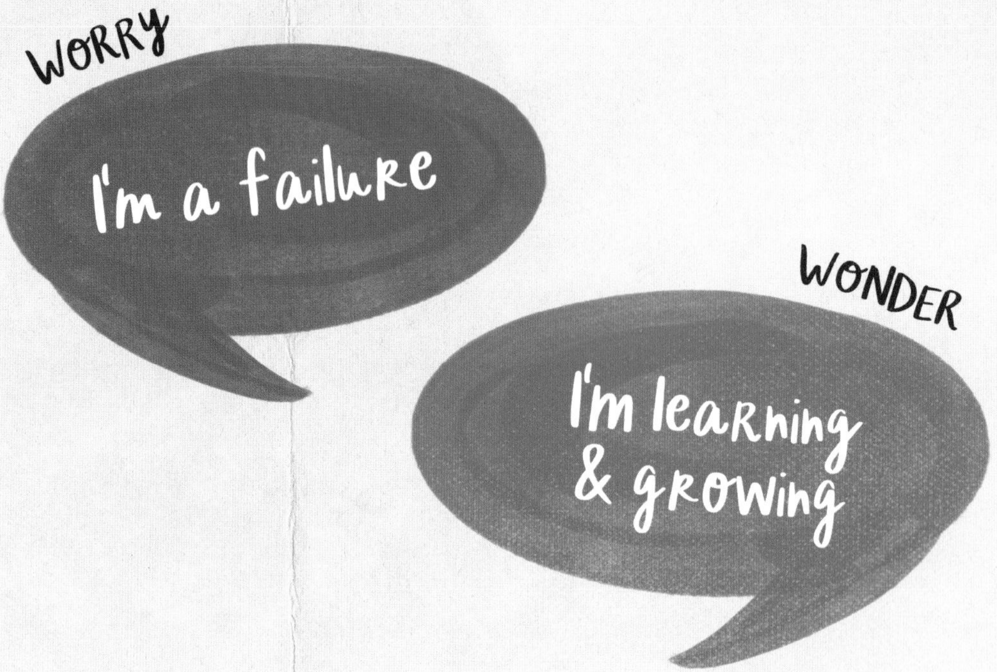

Make More Mistakes

I had the honor of working with legendary marketer and bestselling author Seth Godin many years ago, which instilled in me a key lesson:

Make more mistakes. When we fail quickly and fail often, it's the surest way to learn, grow, and become wiser.

While I've found this to be true, that doesn't always make it comfortable. It can be easy to succumb to the belief that if you make a mistake, either something's wrong with *you* or with the path that you're on.

The truth is: mistakes make up a critically important and unavoidable part of life. They're insights in disguise, bringing us one step closer to where we're meant to go and how we get to grow.

So please remember: mistakes aren't a sign of failure; they're a mark of courage. Each step and *mis*step is a reminder of how brave you are.

Get curious:

What's the last mistake you made?

When you made the mistake, did you celebrate it, learn from it, or judge yourself?

What important lesson did it teach you?

WATCH OUT FOR SHAME

Guilt = I made a mistake

Shame = I'm a mistake

Forgiveness = I'm learning

Wisdom = What did I
learn from this?

Don't Play the Shame Game

The difference between guilt and shame is an important one.

Guilt says, "I did something bad." Shame, on the other hand, says, "*I'm* bad." Guilt says, "I made a mistake," whereas shame says, "*I'm* a mistake."

When we do something that doesn't line up with what we value, guilt helps us course-correct and realign with what matters. It's uncomfortable, but it's useful. Shame, however, has us interpret our mistakes as personal. It's what has us believe that if we mess up or let someone down, it must mean something is wrong with *us*.

I've definitely fallen into many shame spirals in my life—thinking my missteps mean I'm not worthy or lovable—and it's through practicing compassion and forgiveness with myself that I'm able to walk my way out of the spiral and into remembering that worth and love aren't earned, they're inherent.

Can you think of a time when you made an error or mistake, and thought something was wrong with *you*? What loving reminder would you offer a friend who was experiencing the same situation?

As self-compassion researcher Kristin Neff reminds us: "Treat yourself as you would treat a good friend."

Let Compassion Lead the Way

Life doesn't always go according to plan. Messing up, falling short, facing frustration, experiencing loss—this is part of our shared human experience.

When this does inevitably happen, it's important to notice who speaks more: the voice of the critic or the voice of compassion.

The critic is quick to judge and ridicule you for your shortcomings, failures, and inadequacies. The voice of compassion, on the other hand, recognizes that being imperfect, making mistakes, and experiencing difficulty is a vital part of being *human*.

Over the years, I've had many challenging encounters with the critic, and when I notice that voice begin to creep in and take over, I'll pause and ask myself, "What would the voice of compassion say right now?"

When the critic says, "I can't believe you're changing your mind again. You're so unreliable," compassion chimes in to say, "It takes courage to honor what's true. Good for you!"

When the critic says, "I can't believe you messed up. You're such a failure," compassion says, "How *human* of you to make a mistake. Let's celebrate the wisdom and lesson available here. What is this moment teaching you?"

When the critic says, "Stop being so emotional. You should be over this by now," compassion jumps in to say, "I can see this is really difficult for you right now. It's okay to feel hurt. How can you comfort and care for yourself right now?"

As we meet ourselves with kindness, grace, and compassion, it ripples out to our families, our communities, and the world. You were not meant to be perfect or to have it all figured out, love; you were meant to evolve and grow with love.

I invite you to take a moment to consider: What critical voice has been present for you lately? And, what would the voice of compassion have to say?

What Happened	Critic Says	Compassion Says
YOU CHANGE YOUR MIND	"YOU NEVER FOLLOW THROUGH."	"GOOD FOR YOU. HONOR WHAT'S MOST TRUE."
YOU MAKE A MISTAKE	"WHAT'S WRONG WITH YOU?"	"HOW BRAVE! WHAT ARE YOU LEARNING?"
YOU FEEL DOWN	"GET OVER IT. DON'T BE SO SENSITIVE."	"IT'S OKAY TO FEEL THAT WAY!"

When you
doubt your power
↓ you give ↓
power to your doubt

Rise Above Doubt

There will be moments when it's time to put your voice and vulnerability out there. Naturally, as you leave your comfort zone, a number of doubts may come to the surface, like: Will anyone care? Who am I to do this? What will people think of me? Does what I have to say even matter?

Coming from someone who's *very* familiar with that exact set of questions, remember this, love:

Your doubts are often overdramatic and fearful stories. They are not the truth. Rather than view doubt as an enemy, acknowledge that it's trying to keep you safe. I like to say, "Oh, hey there, Doubt, I see you trying to protect me. I appreciate your concern, but I've got this. Get in the back seat; I'm driving."

Remember that experiencing doubt isn't the issue; what matters most is how you respond to the doubt when you feel it.

There are always two choices:

1. Believe it and hide.

2. Or see it and rise.

As van Gogh once said, "If you hear a voice within you say 'You cannot paint,' then by all means paint, and that voice will be silenced."

Let this be an invitation to rise above doubt today.

Stop "Should"-ing Yourself

Time and time again, people ask me, "How do I break free from what other people expect, to create a life that's meaningful to me?"

It starts by becoming aware of the little voice inside your head that tells you what you "should" or "shouldn't" do. "Shoulds" live in a world of right and wrong and good and bad. It's the rules we inherit from family, culture, and society. The rules that breed shame, guilt, and not feeling good enough—and actively keep us from pursuing what we care about most.

When we stop "should"-ing ourselves, we begin to create a life that reflects our values and true desires.

To move beyond "should," notice when that little voice arises, and ask yourself:

Why should I?
Who says so?
Where did I learn this?
What do I truly want?
What tiny, authentic step can I take today?

Above all, remember: let your truest desires lead the way. They will not lead you astray.

Am I Ready Yet?

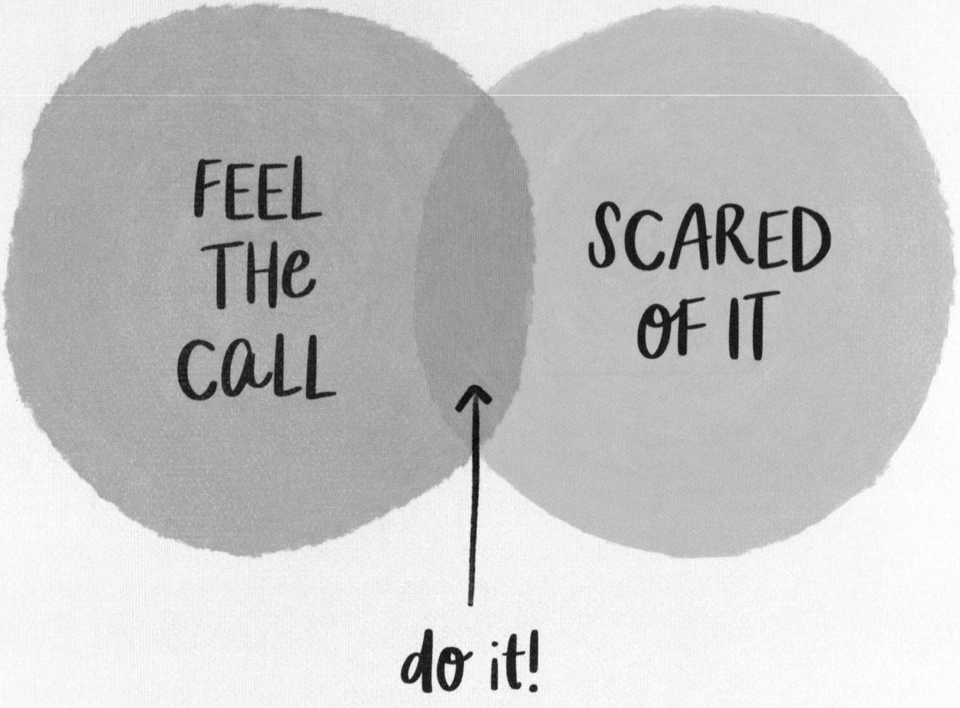

Am I Ready Yet? (Spoiler: You Are)

"Am I ready yet?"

How often have you asked that question—putting off what you truly want in exchange for what feels comfortable and safe?

Generally, when we ask ourselves this question, what we're really asking is:

> Am I ready to face my fears?
>
> Am I ready to act without knowing what happens next?
>
> Am I ready to face naysayers?
>
> Am I ready to *really* trust myself?

The answer to those questions, I've found, is always a wholehearted "yes."

Because on the other side of fear is unimaginable growth and possibility. We can spend our entire lives waiting to be "ready," or we can instill in ourselves a key belief:

I'm as ready as I'll ever be. I'll figure it out as I go—step by step by step.

The next step is already within you. Consider this your invitation to take it.

Your Mess Is Your Message

Consider this: the thing you think you are making a "mess" out of in your life may be the area of learning and growth you were destined for. Perhaps that "mess" is leading you directly to how you can best be a gift to others in this world.

For a long time, I repressed and wronged my emotions. Whenever an unfamiliar or uncomfortable feeling would arise, I would push it aside or pretend I was fine. Over time, I learned the power and freedom in creating space for and embracing all of my emotions.

I began to have conversations with the different emotions living inside of me.

"Fear, what are you here to teach me?"

"Envy, what are you helping me unlock?"

"Joy, how can I create more room for you?"

The more I explored these questions, I realized my "mess"—that initial inability to address my emotions—was my core message.

In the midst of my own exploration, I began to share what I was learning with the world and offer up a bit of medicine to others challenged by their own emotional world, too.

SPEAK YOUR TRUTH. SHARE YOUR MESS. LET YOURSELF BE SEEN.

IT LEADS TO MORE INTIMACY, DEPTH & MEANING—NOT LESS.

What about you? Is there an area of your life that feels "messy"? Is there a part of yourself you tend to conceal or run away from?

Maybe that mess is exactly what you're here for. Maybe that mess is pointing you toward the ways in which you can best be a gift and salve in the world.

Your mess can be your greatest message—if you let it be.

REJECTION IS REDIRECTION

REJECTION IS REDIRECTION

Rejection Is Redirection

We've all been there: feeling the sting of receiving a rejection. Why is rejection, in particular, so unsettling?

It's because rejection triggers the part of our brains responsible for physical pain. When we feel rejected, we literally *feel* rejected. And when we add a story to that feeling, about our worthiness, talents, or lovability, we only amplify and prolong the sensation.

It can be challenging to not take rejection personally, and there have been plenty of times in my life when I made a "no" mean something was wrong with me or my work. What's encouraged me to bounce back is remembering that "rejection is redirection."

Every relationship that hurt me eventually led me to true love. Every career opportunity that I missed out on paved the way for new paths that I never saw coming. Every mistake that gutted me pointed me in the direction of meaningful learning and growth.

Rejection is only one stop on the journey to joy, fulfillment, and success. Beyond what we think we want often lives something even better. Doors need to close for new ones to open. So trust that what's meant for you is ahead—so long as you keep going.

GRATITUDE CHANGES EVERYTHING (REALLY)

Gratitude Changes Everything (Really)

Gratitude is a hot topic these days. People talk about it so much, and here's why it matters:

It can be easy and natural to find fault in life, and gratitude helps you become present to what's important and meaningful.

I read in *The New York Times* that in successful relationships, positive interactions outnumber negative moments by at least five to one. It may not always feel this way since our brains are hardwired to dwell on negativity. This reminds me that for the flaws I can find and point out in life and in my relationships, there are many other things to appreciate and cherish. Remembering that life is fleeting and tomorrow isn't promised, gratitude can help clarify what's worth getting bothered about today.

Let this be an invitation to release what's "wrong" or "not working" for now—and to let gratitude be a shortcut to feeling better.

Check in: What good has happened in your life, and in the world, lately?

Feel Your Uncomfortable Feelings

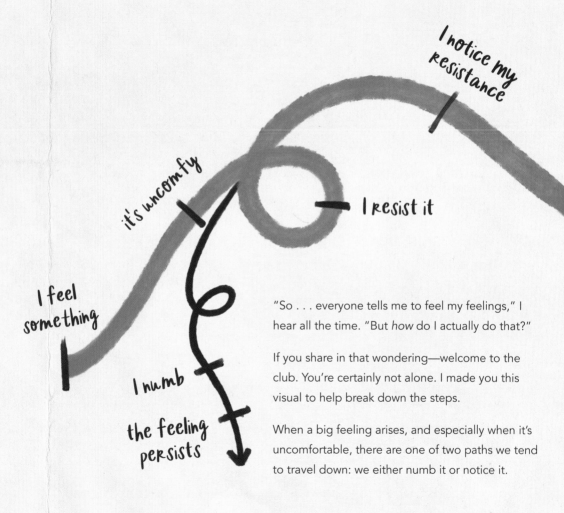

I notice my resistance

it's uncomfy

I resist it

I feel something

I numb

the feeling persists

"So . . . everyone tells me to feel my feelings," I hear all the time. "But *how* do I actually do that?"

If you share in that wondering—welcome to the club. You're certainly not alone. I made you this visual to help break down the steps.

When a big feeling arises, and especially when it's uncomfortable, there are one of two paths we tend to travel down: we either numb it or notice it.

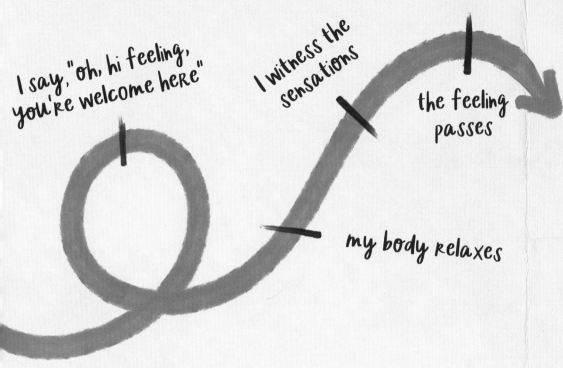

I say, "oh, hi feeling, you're welcome here"

I witness the sensations

the feeling passes

my body relaxes

When we numb an emotion—by ignoring it, pretending it doesn't exist, or making it wrong—we may experience temporary relief, but the feeling will persist, creating even more discomfort.

If we can get into the practice of noticing the feeling and greeting it with curiosity and care, we create the space for the feeling to move through us. If the mental chatter chimes in to say, "I shouldn't feel this way," "This is bad," or "I can't handle this," gently come back to your breath and the sensations in your body.

Breathe. Witness. Allow. Release.

This is a practice, strengthened through trial and error—so be kind with yourself.

A TIP:

RESEARCH SHOWS EMOTIONS MOVE THROUGH OUR SYSTEM IN 6-90 SECONDS. BUT THE STORY WE CREATE? THAT'S WHAT STICKS.

The Ninety-Second Rule

Did you know that the life span of an emotion is around ninety seconds?

Yes. Ninety *seconds*.

So why do emotions sometimes seem to linger for so much longer?

It's because the story we create about the emotion—this is bad, I'm doing this wrong, so-and-so doesn't love me, or I'm not good enough—is what sticks and causes us to endure those uncomfortable (and often unhelpful) feelings even longer. Sometimes for days, weeks, or even *years*.

What's important to recognize is that you are not your feelings; you are the witness of them. Sensations like stress, anxiety, overwhelm, sadness, joy, and anger come and go like weather patterns. The key is learning to not overidentify with or hook into a story about the emotion; instead, observe the emotion gently, with curiosity, and from a distance.

The next time a big feeling comes up, give yourself ninety seconds to breathe, fully feel the sensation, witness the thoughts without attaching to them, and most importantly: let it pass.

As spiritual teacher Lalah Delia says, "This is all temporary. Love yourself through it."

Own the story you create

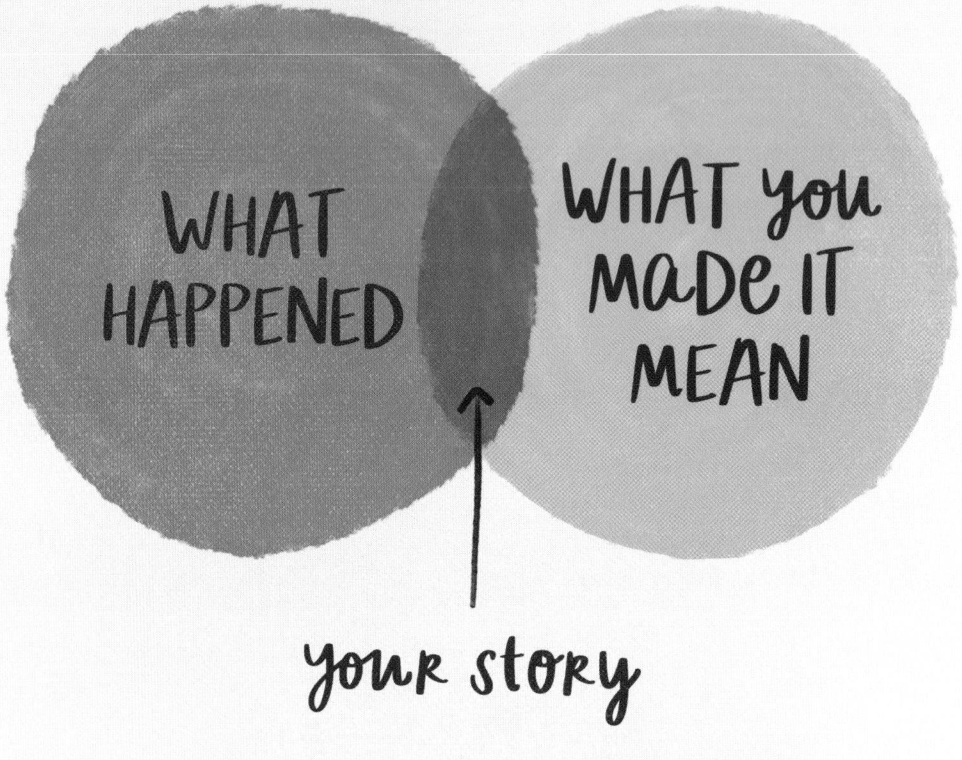

Own the Story You Create

As I once heard my favorite poet, IN-Q, say, "We will always find the evidence for what we choose to believe."

Beliefs and stories grip our lives in powerful ways. Something happens, we draw meaning from it, and that interpretation impacts how we feel and what we choose to believe about ourselves and the world.

When events happen in our lives (e.g., a friend doesn't text us back, someone tells us no, we face conflict with a partner), we tend to interpret and make meaning out of those events (e.g., that friend doesn't care, our work isn't valuable, our partner is losing interest), and then we show up and respond to life as if that's the Truth—with a capital *T*.

To own your story is to take full responsibility for the way you're choosing to interpret what happens in your life. Sometimes the way we interpret situations serves us. Other times, it holds us back. Much of the fear, anxiety, and stress that we experience in everyday life is self-created based on the stories we're choosing to tell ourselves.

Think about it. . . . What have you made a recent experience mean? Is that story serving you? What's another, more true story that you can tell yourself instead?

Triggers Are Teachers

When an event occurs in your life, or someone says something that creates a strong reaction in you, that "trigger" is a powerful teacher.

Instead of resisting the trigger—by becoming defensive or making yourself wrong for experiencing it—practice observing yourself and the situation with neutral curiosity.

You can bring lightness and ease to the situation by saying to yourself, "It's so interesting that I reacted that way when so-and-so said that!" or, "It's so curious that when that happened, I became really defensive."

Neutral curiosity allows us to distance ourselves from the reaction, so that we can look at it as a place we get to grow.

What's a recent moment when you felt triggered? What might that be here to teach you?

Be Soft with Yourself

Years ago, I had a life-changing encounter. I was writing in a wine bar about everything in life that was not going according to plan, when a silver-haired sage with bright blue eyes approached me.

"Is anyone sitting here?"

"No," I replied. "You're welcome to join me."

She smiled, looked at my notebook, and looked at me. "What do you write about?" she asked, with kind eyes and a softness that comforted me like a warm blanket. It felt as if some part of her intuitively knew that I dreamed of being a writer but couldn't muster up the courage to pursue it seriously.

"Well, I'd like to write, but I'm terrified to pursue it," I said. "And honestly, I feel so lost right now. I want to feel clear on my next steps in life, but I don't, and feel like I should. When I look around, it feels like everyone else has it figured out. I'm actually writing about how much I suck."

We both laughed. Then she leaned toward me, placed her hand on my shoulder, and said something I'll never forget:

"Many moons ago, I learned a very important life secret: no one has it figured out, which means, we get to make it up. We can let life be an arduous battle or a dazzling adventure. We're always the ones in charge."

Even though I barely knew this woman, it felt like she was divinely placed on my path to deliver this perfectly timed piece of wisdom. I soaked up her words and the

BEING HARD ON YOURSELF

BEING SOFT WITH YOURSELF

"I'M SO BEHIND." → "WHAT PROGRESS CAN I CELEBRATE?"

"I SHOULDN'T FEEL THIS WAY." → "IT'S SAFE TO FEEL MY FEELINGS."

"UGH... WHY CAN'T I FIGURE THIS OUT?" → "WHAT IS THIS HERE TO TEACH ME?"

"LIFE IS SUCH A BATTLE." → "HOW CAN I APPROACH IT LIKE AN ADVENTURE?"

gentle manner in which she shared them. When it was time for her to go, we hugged goodbye. She looked at me one last time and said, "Be soft with yourself. Being hard won't take you far."

In that moment I realized how much energy I had spent beating myself up, when instead I could soften and embrace where I was at instead. If you too have been extra hard on yourself lately, consider this a reminder to be gentle with yourself and approach this moment with extra love and care.

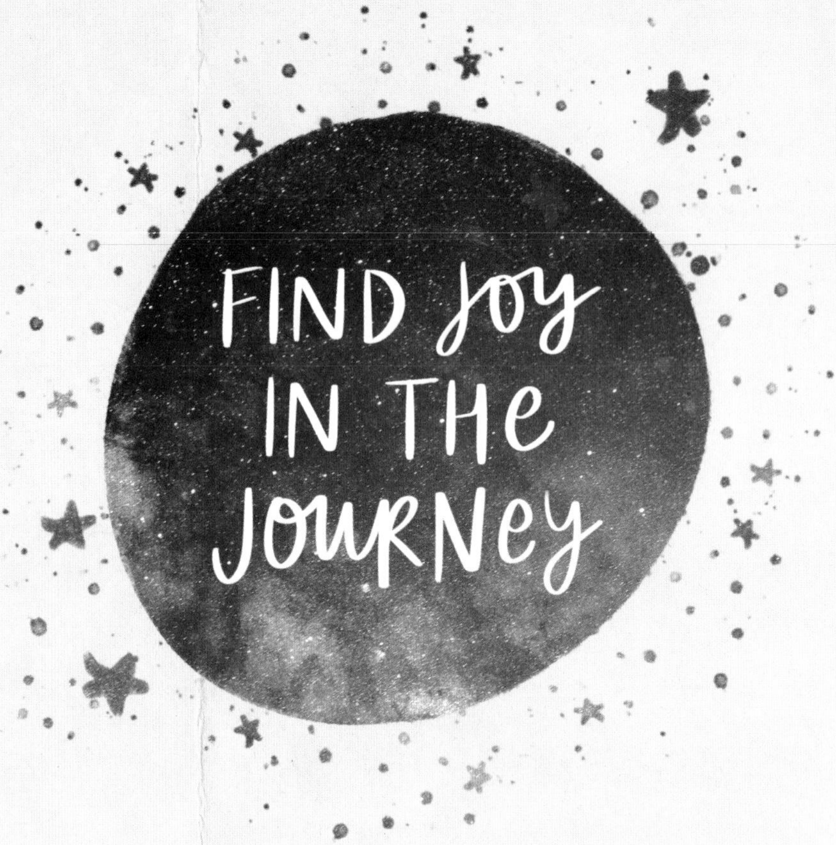
FIND JOY
IN THE
JOURNEY

Find Joy in the Journey

In my many years of creating—whether that's writing books, designing products, creating events, or making art—what I've come to learn is this:

The joy doesn't come just through realizing a goal, crossing a finish line, and getting *there* to the end result. The joy is available right here and now—in every step and *mis*step.

When we fixate on end goals, we may cross a finish line only to realize we were in the wrong race. When we fall in love with the process, and let our curiosity and callings lead the way, our life will unfold in beautiful and often unexpected ways.

Finding joy in the journey will open you up to so much magic, beauty, surprise, and delight. So wherever you're at in your journey, consider this an invitation to appreciate the beauty available in each step.

YOUR INNER CRITIC

IS NOT THE ENEMY

Your Inner Critic Is Not the Enemy

Unpopular opinion: your inner critic is not your enemy.

Yes, the critic might shout nasty things at you, tell you that you're not "doing enough," and try to hijack your happiness. (*Not* cool.)

But what if your critic could also point the path to freedom and peace?

When you really tune in, often your inner critic is pointing you toward one of two things: a story that is no longer serving you, or a wake-up call to make some changes.

Take a moment to tune in: Is your inner critic telling you something that makes you feel small, scared, worthless, or hopeless? If so, it's time to get curious about where that story originated and, perhaps if you're ready, transform it into something more truthful and uplifting.

Or is your inner critic telling you something that actually feels true and helpful, but is hard to hear? If so, perhaps it's time to integrate a small change into your life to move you in a more aligned direction.

Whatever you discover, remember that your inner critic can be a helpful teammate, reminding you when it's time to release, hold on to, or transform something in your life.

Find Your Grace

Early in my creative journey, I struggled moving projects along because nothing was ever "good enough" according to my inner perfectionist. I had such a contentious relationship with this part of me that I decided to give her a name. Or rather, she decided to name herself.

"You may call me Grace," she said one day, in her elegant English accent. Grace wasn't afraid to speak up and call out what didn't meet her standards, which, to my sensitive inner artist, felt terrifying and stifling.

	PARALYZING PERFECTIONISM	HEALTHY STRIVING
MISTAKES =	I'm flawed	I'm growing
UNCERTAINTY =	I'm doing it wrong	I'm finding my way
ASKING FOR HELP =	I'm not enough	Better, together
YOUR WORK =	Never good enough	Evolving and improving
FLAWS =	Unlovable	Human

Over time, I got curious about Grace's hopes and fears, as well as what my sensitive inner artist needed to feel safe. Hearing and holding space for both parts of me created a more constructive environment.

Now, whenever we're embarking on an important adventure, Grace, the inner artist, and I sit down and have a chat. We create a few ground rules, such as the following:

1. Progress over perfection. We focus on daily experiments over daily masterpieces.

2. Artist mode versus editor mode. Grace's input isn't welcome while in messy artist first-draft mode. This stage of the process is far too sensitive and needs to be handled with extra care. Grace is most useful later—when editing and shaping the work.

3. Connect before correct. We ask Grace to share what resonates with her first before she moves into critique. This helps my inner artist see what's working before seeing what needs work.

And when Grace gets bold and lively—which inevitably happens—I remind her of our agreements, and we all get back to work.

Get curious: Is there a challenging voice that's been on repeat for you lately? If so, what might you name it? What does it look and sound like? What agreements can you create to work more playfully and constructively together?

Tap into Flow

Maybe you've experienced flow state at some point—the feeling of being "in the zone." It's when you're singularly focused on something you care deeply about. The mind's chatter fades, time feels like it slows down, and distractions are a non-issue. It feels like the dots connect and click, and you feel spellbound. It's my favorite feeling in the world.

Popularized by psychologists Mihaly Csikszentmihalyi and Jeanne Nakamura, this chart is a re-creation of their brilliant work on creativity and flow.

Getting to a state of flow is not so much about being relaxed and receptive; it's when you're being stretched and challenged toward a worthwhile pursuit—and that activity is what you enjoy and are good at.

There are two parts of this chart that I find particularly useful in the creative process (and for life in general):

1. When I'm moving into boredom—because the activity isn't enjoyable or challenging enough. That's an opportunity to ask myself: What risk I can take or what constraint I can create to challenge myself?

2. What I'm moving into anxiety—because the activity is *too* challenging or I don't have enough experience. That's an opportunity to ask myself: How can I adjust what I'm doing to fit within my skill set, or what new skills do I need to learn here?

Finding that sweet spot of flow is about mastering skills that matter to you, while also pursuing projects and opportunities that highlight your talents and challenge you in a meaningful way.

Think about your own flow: What step can you take today to access flow state?

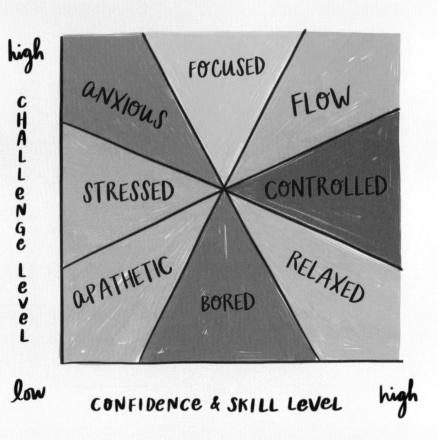

DOES THIS LIGHT ME UP?

NAH. → LET IT GO.

KIND OF. → TABLE IT.

YASSS! → DO IT!

* INSPIRED BY DEREK SIVERS

Do What Lights You Up

There are moments in our lives when it's important to do things we don't *really* want to do—because those things are meaningful to us. But far too often, I hear stories of people *continually* investing their time in activities that *don't* light them up, but instead bring them down. Why?

It happens when we carry beliefs like:

"It can't be easy or feel good."

"If I'm not struggling, I'm not growing."

"This is how other people are doing it, so I should, too."

"It's too hard to change."

"This is just the way things are."

I too catch myself falling into cycles of not trusting what feels good and thinking that if it's not hard, it's not worthwhile.

This simple check-in—Does this light me up?—has done wonders for helping me create a life that reflects who I am, what I value, and what brings me joy. I hope it does the same for you too.

GET CURIOUS
What *truly* lights you up?

You DON'T
HAVE To
SuFFeR To
MAKe ART

You Don't Have to Suffer to Make Art

One of the biggest lies we tell ourselves is that we need to suffer in order to make art.

And when I say "art," I'm not talking exclusively about the creative arts. I'm referring to creating anything that *moves* you. From spreadsheets to song lyrics, sculptures to sales emails—art forms are all around us. So you do *you*.

A pain point I often hear from artists is that they think they need to burn themselves out to cross a finish line, work with demanding clients to test their will, or show up at the same time and place every day to force the art out—no matter what.

While being disciplined, embracing discomfort, and pushing your edges are useful tools in the creative process, that doesn't mean that suffering is the only way to create great art. A question you might consider is: If I remembered that the point of making art is to be *moved* by the process, how might I design my day and week?

Perhaps your art will come out with greater ease when you spend less time in front of a screen and more time with pen and paper. Maybe you're more creative outside the hours of 9 to 5. Perhaps a desk is less your thing, and you create with more inspiration in bed. Maybe guided prompts will help get you started—or maybe it's best to freewrite or draw or take a walk through nature at the start of each session, with no expectations in mind.

Whatever it is for you, consider this an invitation to bring joy and play into your creative process, just as much as structure and devotion. As renowned creativity teacher Julia Cameron says, "Serious art comes from serious play."

Create Magic That Resonates

Here are the sweet spots I've found in creating things that resonate:

It's personal. When you go through the process of making your insides and vulnerabilities visible, that is often where some of your best, most authentic work will come to the surface. When you're brave enough to channel your fears, insecurities, and curiosities into what you create, it makes others feel like they aren't alone in their lives.

It's universal. While the details in each of our stories may look different, we can all relate to the same set of emotions. You'd be hard-pressed to find someone who has not also experienced grief, joy, envy, anxiety, awe, and fear. It's easy to think we are unique and alone in feeling, thinking, and behaving the way we do—but what's personal to you is universal to all.

It's a little uncomfy. Strive to make work that makes you a little uncomfortable. Not so uncomfortable that you're not making progress, but just enough that you're pushing your edges. Try something new, something you're not sure will work. The mystery is what keeps things interesting.

GET CURIOUS

What are you aching to create that lives at the interaction of these three elements for you?

UNIVERSAL

A LIL' UNCOMFY

DEEPLY PERSONAL

MAGIC

Let Yourself Be Seen

When I first started public-speaking, I was terrified. I'd obsessively practice and memorize my lines, speak really fast to get it over with, and exhale with relief the second it was over.

One time, after an event, a woman approached me and said, "I love what you have to say, but can you slow down a bit? You're not letting us see you."

You're not letting us see you.

Her words hit me like a ton of bricks. All along, I thought I was terrified of speaking. But what I was really afraid of was being seen and being judged.

Recognizing this, I wondered: What will it take for me to see myself, to accept myself, and to love the parts of me that I'm struggling to love?

An interesting pattern emerged: as I became more comfortable in my skin, I felt more comfortable onstage. As I learned to celebrate and embrace my imperfections, I worried less about others judging me. The stage and the audience were a mirror for how I was relating to myself.

Take a moment to tune in and ask yourself: Is there a part of you that you're still hiding? A part of you that aches to be seen?

Consider this an invitation to let yourself be seen. Not everyone will deserve to see you, of course. But when you allow yourself to be *truly* seen, first by yourself, and then by those who matter most—it can liberate you in profound ways.

Above all, I want you to know: you are seen and loved for *all* of who you are. I don't need to know you to know this. You are worthy of being seen. You are worthy of being loved. This moment, the next, and always.

COURAGE REQUIRES FEAR

Courage Requires Fear

Many people tell me that they want to be more courageous. But the thing we often don't realize about courage is that it *requires* fear. In other words, if you ask for more courage in your life, don't be surprised if you begin to attract situations that evoke fear in you.

Whether the fear arises around speaking your truth, showing up as who you truly are, or making an important change in your life, fear is not an emotion to overcome but one to dance with.

When Fear says, "This is scary and I don't want to go there," Courage says, "We've got this. Let's take the next step." Courage takes Fear's hand and walks in the direction of what's right and true.

So go where there is fear—and let your courageousness lead the way toward what's important and meaningful to *you*.

INTUITION V. FEAR

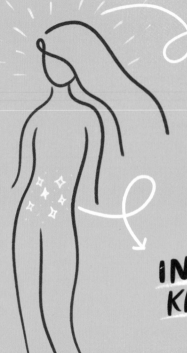

FEAR & ANXIETY

NEEDS

- 5-MINUTE MEDITATION
- FAITH & TRUST
- TINY STEPS FORWARD
- TO BE ACKNOWLEDGED

INTUITION & KNOWING

NEEDS

- QUIET & SPACE
- SOLO TIME IN NATURE
- DAILY JOURNALING
- TO BE HONORED

Discern Fear from Intuition

When we're faced with an opportunity to expand and evolve, it's natural to feel hesitant or torn. Learning to detect the difference between fear that's trying to stop you and intuition that's here to support you is an important skill set.

We can learn to discern fear from intuition by tuning in to the wisdom of our body.

Fear is loud, anxious, and often includes a lot of fast-moving thoughts. It's focused on the past and future and tends to feel restrictive or stifling. While fear is ultimately trying to keep you safe, it can also prevent you from moving in the direction of what's meaningful and true. When fear arises, you can ask: What do you need, Fear, to feel safe? Once Fear feels seen, it tends to create space for a wiser part of us to speak up.

Intuition feels like a clear knowing felt from deep within. Intuition isn't focused on the past or future; it's intent on the present. Intuition may come in the form of a quiet, gentle whisper or "hunch" felt in your body. Other times, it may shout "NO" to get your attention, signal danger, or help you avoid making misaligned decisions.

To access the wisdom of your intuition, consider the question that's in your heart. Then, take a few deep breaths, close your eyes, and tune in:

Does this choice feel contracting or expansive?

Does saying "yes" cause me to feel delight or dread?

If money wasn't a consideration, would I still say "yes"?

Move toward what feels true, expansive, and more like an opening—even if it isn't necessarily easy, straightforward, or devoid of risk.

Afraid of Judgment? Speak Up Anyway

So many people hesitate to express their truth out of fear of being judged by others. It can be especially scary to share in public—like in a blog or social media post—for fear of how people will respond.

The reality is whenever you share your truth—whether in a private one-on-one conversation, or on the internet with thousands of people—you are giving people something to respond to, whether or not you want the response.

It's important to remember a few things whenever you share your truth with others:

1. You cannot control how people perceive you, and if they judge you. Trying to do so is almost always a waste of energy.

2. You will be judged. Not everyone will resonate with or even understand what you have to say, and that's okay. When you let go of trying to win everyone over, you take the pressure off and learn to show up as yourself, for yourself, instead.

(And let's be honest: Do you resonate with everyone? I didn't think so.)

If concern about feeling judged is keeping you from sharing your important truths, here are a few helpful questions you can ask yourself:

WHAT IF THEY JUDGE ME?

FEAR

Let's play it safe.

COURAGE

They may. Let's speak up anyway.

Even if I am judged, is it worth speaking up anyway?

What might I gain? What must I say? And who will benefit?

Remember: the only thing you can control is what you share and how you share it, but not how other people ultimately choose to receive it.

Transform Your Thoughts

Your thoughts have enormous power.

They have the power to change how you feel, how much energy you have, what action you take (or don't take), and how you relate to those around you.

Think of a thought you've had on repeat lately that doesn't make you feel very good. Maybe you've been telling yourself:

- I'm a mess
- I can't do this
- I'm a failure
- I'm scared

- I don't know how I am going to overcome this situation

Here's what reframing that thought could sound like:

- I'm human
- I can do hard things
- I'm learning
- I'm safe

- Things will work out, even if I can't see a clear path forward just yet

It's okay if you don't fully feel the truth of these reframes right away. Simply give yourself an opportunity to try them on for size and see how they feel. The aim here isn't to ignore what's difficult; it's to look for what's *also* true.

Your thoughts are always guiding you toward the future version of yourself. Whenever possible, choose the thoughts that guide you closer to who you hope to become.

Let Your Feelings Be Friends

All of your emotions play an important role in the ever-unfolding story that is your life.

Many of us try to boost the "good" feelings (like joy, love, calm, excitement, and peace) while eliminating the "bad" feelings (like envy, guilt, shame, anxiety, or sadness).

But your feelings are not good *or* bad. They are simply wise messengers that lead the way to living life as your whole, authentic self.

The more you position some emotions as "good" and others as "bad," the more you consciously (and often unconsciously) try to chase the former and suppress the latter.

What if all of your emotions could work in concert, creating a symphony that adds richness, depth, self-understanding, and empathy to your life? What if all of your emotions could be friends?

I write a lot about listening to your emotions and the wisdom they want to share with you. But if you are having trouble tapping into those conversations with your inner self, here is something that might help:

Create an actual "box for emotions." In it, put something in the box that represents each feeling you've experienced lately (e.g., sadness, anxiety, joy, envy, excitement, love).

Let your feelings be friends

Keep the box nearby, and whenever you feel called to do so, open it up to get in touch with a specific emotion. Hold the talisman for that emotion in your hand, journal about it, meditate on it.

Over time, you'll get to witness your feelings becoming friends.

OVERWHELMED?
A HELPFUL CHECKLIST

- ☐ RELAX SHOULDERS
- ☐ THREE BREATHS
- ☐ DANCE
- ☐ LIST TOP 3 PRIORITIES

- ☐ TAKE A BREAK
- ☐ GO FOR A WALK
- ☐ ADJUST SCHEDULE
- ☐ ASK FOR HELP

Overwhelmed? A Helpful Checklist

Life feeling like a bit much lately?

Take a deep breath and remember that overwhelm is a stepping stone that helps you expand into your power. Rather than think, "Yikes, this is too much," Overwhelm invites you to consider, "This is new for me, and I'm growing."

Here's a helpful checklist to help you let go of the past, trust the future, and center in the present moment.

Remember: you can handle this.

Energy Is Your Compass

Your energy serves as a compass, guiding you toward what you need physically, emotionally, mentally, and spiritually.

Tune in: What's been draining you lately?

When something is draining, you may feel lethargic, uninspired, low on energy, or even hopeless. When something is energizing, on the other hand, your tone of voice changes when you talk about it. It's easier to enter a flow state. Work, relationships, and projects feel effortless, and time flies by.

When you prioritize your time and attention based on what is the most energizing and engaging, that is when you will tend to experience boundless joy and accomplish your most meaningful work.

By simply paying attention to your energy levels today, you can start to discern between what drains you and what energizes you—and then begin to make small choices that increase the uplifting energy in your life.

The next time you notice your energy dip, ask yourself: What would make this more energizing?

Let energy be your compass toward fulfillment and freedom.

CREATIVITY

NEEDS

SPACE

to

BREATHE

Creativity Needs Space to Breathe

I sat down to write this piece when I was feeling overwhelmed, exhausted, and a little on edge. Guess how far I got?

Not far *at all*. I wrote and deleted, wrote and deleted, trying to force myself to just "get it done." The irony, of course, was that I was being invited to live the message of giving creativity space to breathe before I could sit down to write about it.

So I turned to my inner muse and asked, "What do you need right now?"

"Turn off your phone, go on a walk, and then run a bath," she said. "Once you've taken care of yourself, the words will come."

I share this story as an example of how in our desire to be "productive," we may lose sight of what we need in order to be human.

Creativity isn't linear, can't be forced, and needs space to unfold. It's an ongoing dance of tuning in and listening, and honoring what our inner muse most wants and needs. When we take care of our minds, bodies, and souls, creativity tends to come with more ease.

Sometimes, like today, the muse will tell me to take a break and take care. Other times she'll encourage me to revisit a story and go deeper. Still other times she'll invite me to playfully explore a curiosity.

If you're feeling creatively stuck, have a conversation with your muse. Say, "Hello, Inner Muse. What do you most want and need from me today?" Trust the wisdom that follows, even if it feels unnatural at first.

COME BACK HOME

Come Back Home

It's okay if . . .There's a lot going on.

You can't handle everything this week.

You're feeling tired.

Right now feels like a lot.

You need more time to yourself.

It's okay, love.

Take the space you need. Be kind to yourself. Come back home to yourself before giving more to the world.

Let Go of Toxic Hustle

We live in a world (particularly in the West) that promotes "hustle" culture, gives social status to those who are the most "busy," and ties self-worth to accomplishment.

It is so ingrained in many of us that we don't even realize the present hum of anxiety we feel about "getting more things done."

This doesn't mean hustle is "wrong" or "bad," though it's important to recognize the difference between healthy and toxic hustle.

Healthy hustle looks and feels like this:

Challenging yourself to grow, moving beyond your comfort zone, and committing fully to your vision and values. It's rising in the face of adversity, knowing when to rest and play, and seeing downtime as productive.

Toxic hustle looks and feels like this:

Grinding all day and night, prioritizing work above all else, and grasping and clinging out of a place of lack. It's wearing productivity like a badge of honor, ignoring your body's needs, and forcing outcomes at all costs.

The latter is often the result of a toxic culture or unaddressed fears about worthiness. ("If I achieve _____, I'll be enough.") It can harm your physical and emotional health and often leads to burnout.

Toxic hustle isn't a sustainable path to realizing your dreams. Often, it can hold you back and make you sick. In a culture of getting ahead and always seeking more, taking care of yourself is a radical and necessary act.

Where do you sit on the spectrum of toxic and healthy hustle? What's one way you can promote healthier hustle in your life starting today?

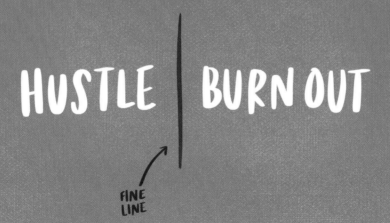

HUSTLE | BURN OUT

FINE
LINE

TO-DO:

☐ REST

☐ REST

☐ REST

Rest *Is* Productive

It's time we broaden our perspective of what it means to be "productive."

Taking a long walk is productive. Calling someone you love is productive. So is writing in a journal, reading a book, or even enjoying that TV show you adore.

One of the biggest lessons I've learned in my own life over the past several years is this:

Rest *is* productive.

Sometimes, the most productive thing is to get a good night's sleep, turn off the phone, or do nothing at all. As I've come to discover, the true measure of productivity isn't found in the number of things I accomplish; it's found in the moments that enrich my life and create meaning.

Take a moment to consider all the things that add great value to your life, including those that society may not deem "productive." Let that list guide the way to a more evolved version of fulfillment and success.

As philosopher Alan Watts reminds us, "Stop measuring days by degree of productivity and start experiencing them by degree of presence."

SUCCESS

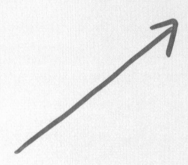

FANTASY

REALITY

The Fantasy of Success

When we imagine our own successful futures, many of us picture a straight line that goes up and to the right. Little by little, we'll climb the ladder, accomplishing our biggest goals in record-breaking time with relative ease.

The reality is that success is a winding, nonlinear, sometimes messy journey. At some point, all of us feel lost, confused, stagnant, or unsuccessful. These feelings are a natural part of the human journey.

What's more, these feelings often have less to do with our actual results and more to do with our expectations about the neat and easy fantasy of success.

When you're feeling like success is out of reach, re-center by asking yourself these questions:

What does success *feel* like on my own terms?

What is this current challenge, setback, or lesson teaching me about my own definition of success?

What is there to celebrate about this moment in my journey?

Creating success and fulfillment may not look the way you think it will. The reality can feel messy and jumbled. But in the end, you'll be able to reflect back and see that the winding road was leading you somewhere meaningful all along.

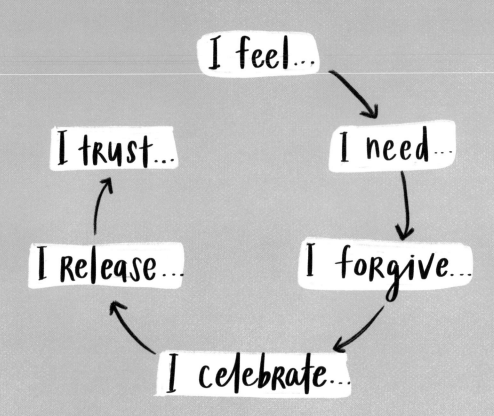

Check In with Yourself

Touching base with yourself every day helps you stay in tune with how you're feeling and what you need, with what there is to appreciate, let go of, and trust. Especially when life is moving quickly, taking just five minutes to check in can make a world of a difference for your mental and emotional well-being.

Tune in: take a few moments to answer the prompts in this check-in tool. You can respond to them mentally or through writing in a journal. Whatever answers come up for you, remember to practice being gentle and compassionate with yourself.

To create a ritual out of checking in, I recommend using this tool in the morning, alongside a habit you already have (like drinking coffee, journaling, or eating breakfast) as a way to connect with yourself before you greet the day.

I also enjoy using these prompts at the end of the week with my team as a way to see where they're at and how they're feeling.

Remember: when you pour into yourself, you can pour more into others.

Live
life on
your terms

signed: _N____

Live Life on Your Terms

We all come up against this eventually: the moment when someone tells us how we "should" live our lives. Maybe it's someone in your family. Maybe it's your friend, a partner, or even a stranger on the internet.

Hearing someone's unsolicited advice on what they think we ought to do with our lives can feel off-putting. I know that when I began breaking free of "shoulds" to create a life that reflected my values and true self, I initially had a really hard time discerning between my own truth and other people's expectations. It would sometimes take me days or weeks to quiet the noise of the external world and return to my own inner voice.

If you find yourself here, remember this:

This is your one life, and you get to live it in precisely the way that you want. You don't need other people to see what you see—and often, people won't ever be able to.

Get very quiet and still and ask yourself one very important question: What is right and true *for me*?

Let that question lead you to create a life on your terms—where the only approval needed is your own.

WHEN WE REACT

EVENT   REACTION

WHEN WE RESPOND

EVENT PAUSE RESPONSE

Honor the Pause

We've all been there—reacting with anger to an offhand comment, reacting with spite when a friend says something hurtful, becoming defensive in the heat of the moment.

When we react, it's instinctual and knee-jerk. It's doing or saying without thinking or without considering the consequences of our actions. It tends to be defensive or protective in nature.

A response adds a deep breath and a pause—a mindful moment to ensure that our actions are lining up with our values.

If you notice yourself on the verge of reacting today, pause and consider: How would my wiser self respond to this?

yes no yes No yes no yes
No Yes no maybe yes No
maybe NO yes NO yes
No yes MAYBE Yes NO
yes no yes no NO maybe
yes no yes No yes no yes
No Yes no maybe yes No
maybe NO yes NO yes
No yes MAYBE Yes NO
yes no yes no NO maybe
yes no yes No yes no

It's Okay to Change Your Mind

Is there something you once said "yes" to that now feels more like a "no" or "not like this"?

I used to be afraid to say "yes" to things for fear that my priorities, curiosities, and truths might change down the road. But here's what I've learned:

You are always and forever allowed to change your mind.

When something no longer feels like it fits in your life, it can be a beautiful sign of your own evolution and self-attunement. As your life changes, your mind also changes about what you want to allow to take up space in your life.

What immediately comes to mind when you think about what isn't working right now?

What change(s) can you make to feel more aligned and free?

Celebrate Your Progress

We live in a culture of more—where there will always be more to learn, to do, to consume, to experience.

The speed at which the world communicates, creates, and moves is increasing, but we still have the same number of hours in a day to work with.

Bearing this reality in mind, you may inevitably start to ask yourself: Am I behind?

While you may never fully get through your to-do list, and you may never accomplish everything you set out to do in this one lifetime—that doesn't mean you're behind. It simply means you're a human with a limited amount of time.

Instead of asking, Am I behind? a more empowering question to ask is, What progress can I celebrate?

What have you done, shared, created, or experienced that you are proud of? What steps forward have you taken? What important lessons have you learned?

On any given day of your life, there's much to celebrate.

From time to time, put your to-do list down and allow yourself to soak up the joy of all the progress you've made.

It'll help you realize that all along—you've been right on time.

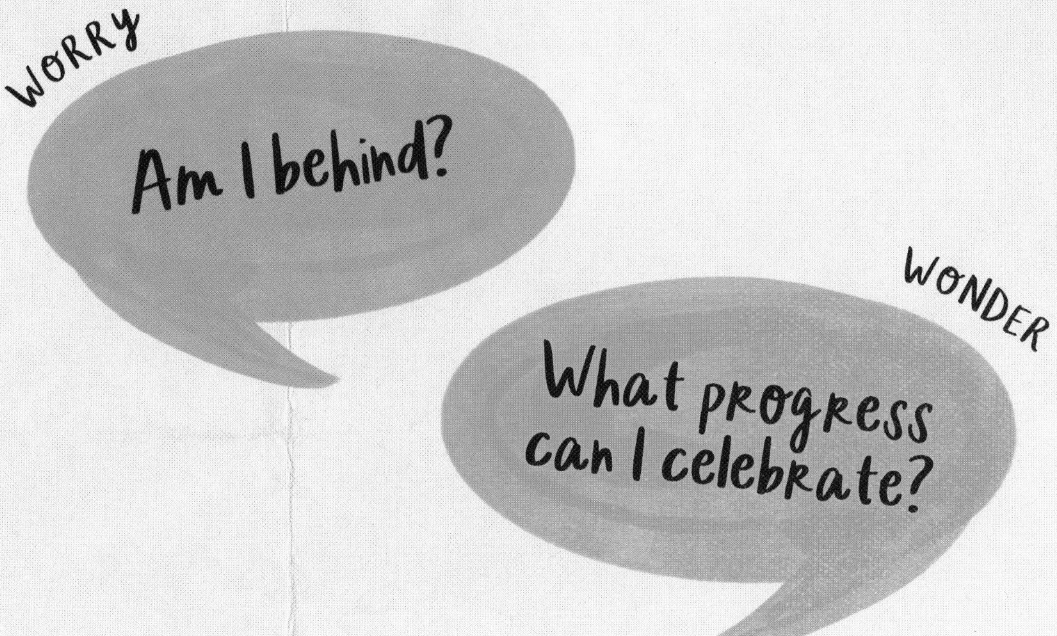
WORRY
Am I behind?
WONDER
What progress can I celebrate?

the right
things?
↓

Am I doing ~~enough~~?

Do What Matters Most

You know that nagging feeling that we're not doing enough and should be doing more? Where does it come from?

Is it brought on by scrolling through social media? A feeling that we have potential untapped? A fear of being left behind? Or our society's obsession with doing *more*?

Sometimes *more* is pointing us toward something important that we're putting off or avoiding. Other times, it's leading us into a bottomless pit of striving, reaching, and proving that we're worthy and enough.

A helpful alternative to doing more is doing what's *meaningful*. Because if your life is a reflection of what's truly important to you, I hope you find comfort in this truth:

You are doing more than enough, because you are doing what matters most to you.

Heck yes! Keep DOING you.
BUT WHY DO I Keep DOUBTING?!
Because you're HUMAN AND you CARe.
WHAT IF I MAKe A WRONG CHOICe?
WRONG WILL LeAD you TO RIGHT.
ARe you SURe?!
THeRe IS NO ONe "RIGHT" PATH. CLARITY COMeS THROUGH ALIGNeD ACTION.

Trust the Process

We've all been there—that moment when you experience uncertainty and discomfort.

Maybe you are feeling unsure about something relatively small, like not knowing the answer to a question. Or perhaps you are experiencing the unsettling feeling of not knowing what to do in regards to a bigger decision:

Should you stay in your current relationship?

Is it time to make a career leap?

Can you create healthy boundaries without isolating people you love?

In ways big and small, we're faced with many moments of uncertainty in our lives. These moments can spark fear, scarcity, and anxiety—and have us feel confused about our right next step.

As my friend and entrepreneur Dhru Purohit says, "Confusion is not knowing, but needing to know. The 'needing' changes everything; the needing is where the anxiety and stress come from."

How might things look differently if you surrendered your need to know and trusted that clarity would soon come?

Consider this an invitation to embrace uncertainty and stay open to what this moment is here to teach you. Your uncertainty may very well be the path leading you directly to a truer, fuller, and freer future.

Trust the process.

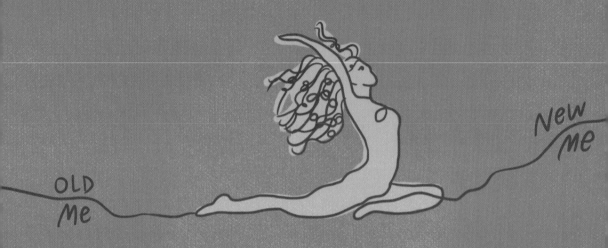

Embrace the In-Between

Life is not a linear path. It's filled with ebbs, flows, twists, turns, and many moments of "in-between." When we find ourselves someplace unexpected, we may be inclined to think, "This is bad," "I don't like this," or "This shouldn't be happening this way, or to me."

But what if this exact moment was ultimately serving the purpose of bringing you toward a more evolved and whole version of yourself? What if the uncertainties you're facing at this very moment are important steps on your journey toward a more aligned version of you?

Sometimes the things you hope for end up being the things you're glad you didn't get. Other times, the challenges you face and discomfort you feel lead you directly or indirectly to the most rewarding experiences, people, and discoveries of your life.

What is meant for you will always find you, at exactly the time it needs to—as long as you stay open to and, to the best of your ability, embrace this moment fully.

So whenever you find yourself caught in the thinking that you aren't where you ought to be, remember that you are a caterpillar on one leaf on one tree in a vast forest. You will not always understand what is happening around you, and sometimes you may not even understand your own metamorphosis.

But, always, you are becoming something bigger, truer, and more beautiful than what you already are in this moment. In the calm, as well as in the chaos. Look around for the beauty; you may find it in the most unexpected of places.

THE LIGHT WAY IS THE

RIGHT WAY

The Light Way Is the Right Way

When we look for the lighter path, it can help us navigate challenges with more grace, trust, and inner peace.

When a project is feeling heavy, for example, and I'm procrastinating, overthinking, or avoiding the situation, I'll tune inward and ask:

How can I make this more easeful? Enjoyable? Light? What can I do to lighten the load?

When I'm choosing between a few possible paths and I'm not clear on which way to go, I'll tune in to the wisdom of my body and notice:

Which of these options feels light and expansive? Where do I feel an opening and an ease? Where do I feel myself pulled?

When I'm arguing with my mom, and all I really want is to feel aligned and connected, I'll pause and wonder:

How can I bring lightness to this situation? Where can I be more gentle with myself and with him?

Looking for the lighter path doesn't mean we ignore what's difficult, challenging, or heavy. It means we show up for and respond to those moments with more curiosity, compassion, and ease.

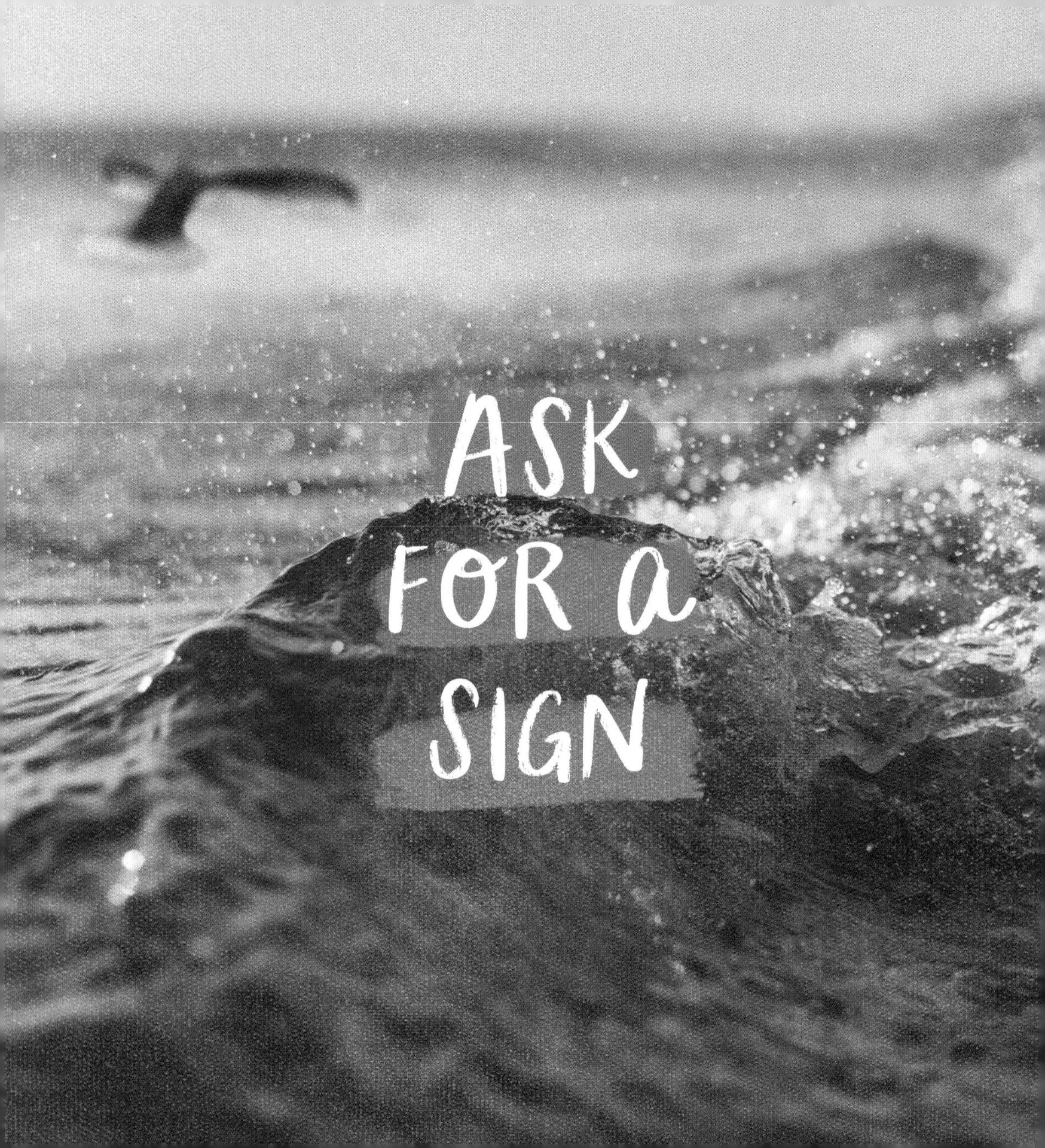
ASK
FOR a
SIGN

Ask for a Sign

When I was in grief around the sudden disappearance of my beloved cat Luna, a psychic medium recommended that I ask for a very specific sign so that the universe could communicate with me. Hearing her suggestion brought about two reactions at once: one part of me felt a sense of wonder and awe, while another part of me tried not to roll my eyes with disbelief.

Feeling ever so slightly more curious than skeptical, I asked the universe to show me a purple dolphin. ("Good luck finding a purple dolphin!" my inner skeptic sneered.) The next day, while driving, a mural I had never seen before with two purple dolphins came into my line of sight. I gasped, screamed with delight, and then cried.

And thus began my adventures in asking the universe for signs. We can ask for signs when we're feeling unsure about a decision, wanting confirmation that we're on the right path, or when we're at the end of our rope around a situation. As I learned from medium Laura Lynne Jackson, when choosing a sign, let it be specific and unique for you, but try not to overthink it. Trust the first thing that comes to mind. It could be an animal, a number sequence, a song, or an image.

When asking for a sign, I'll say, "Dear universe, I need your help. Please show me my sign if . . ." Then I'll release my grip and surrender to something bigger than me.

Sometimes the sign reveals itself quickly; other times, it can take days or weeks. Sometimes it never shows, and that in itself, can be a sign, too. I find it helpful to remember that the noise and clutter of modern life can prevent us from seeing or registering our signs—so to remember to practice presence.

Above all, the invitation here is to open your heart to receiving guidance and to allow the mysteries of the universe to communicate with you.

What sign will you ask for today?

It's all about perspective.

DAYS & WEEKS

MONTHS & YEARS

Find Perspective

There are moments in our lives when we may feel centered, in flow, clear, and productive. It feels as if we are flowing with the river of life; there is an easefulness, a feeling of forward motion, a sense of awe.

And then there are the moments when we're thrust into so much uncertainty and the unknown that we struggle to find our center. Days and weeks may feel like a roller coaster with no end in sight. We may wonder how we got here and how we'll make it through.

It's only later, through the gift of perspective, that we may realize how the obstacles and challenges we faced were leading us exactly where we needed to go in order to grow.

Trust the ebbs and flows of your journey. Rather than grasping for control or trying to force certainty, try to witness the unfolding of your life with as much curiosity and perspective as you can muster. You may discover that it helps you find magic in the mess, and treasure in the even most trying of times.

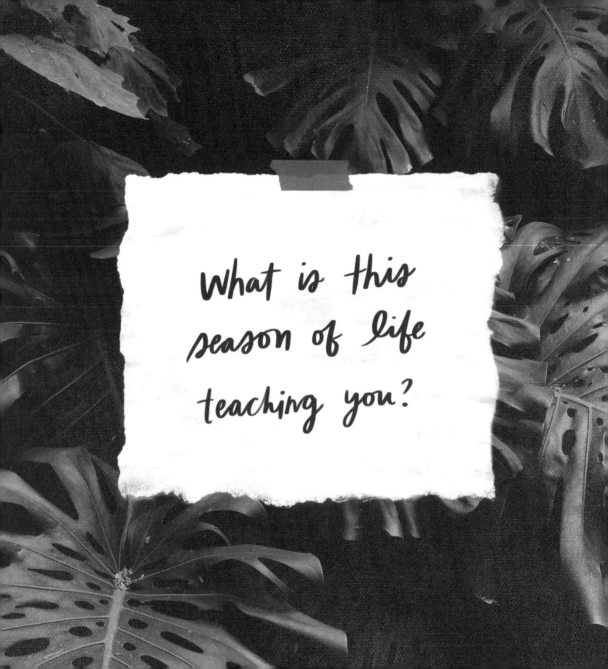

Reflect on This Season's Story

As a writer, I tend to view life through the lens of a storyteller. We are all the heroes and heroines of our lives, going through deep inner transformation—again and again and again.

As I learned from legendary mythologist Joseph Campbell and what he calls the Hero's Journey, the (very simplified) adventure looks something like this:

I feel a call to adventure that takes me away from my ordinary world. I face trials and tribulations, breakdowns and breakthroughs. I learn to slay inner dragons and ultimately return with a treasure to bring wisdom back to the ordinary world.

I find this story structure to be immensely helpful, especially when it feels like I'm in the middle of a storm. It helps me remember, "Oh, I'm in the breakdown part right now before the breakthrough. The breakthrough is coming." And it always does.

Your invitation for today is to reflect on the story of this season of your life.

1. If your life was a book, what would you call it?

2. What would the title of your current chapter be?

3. What is the inherent lesson or gift that this moment in your life has to offer?

~~Is this true?~~

Is this useful?

Question Your Thoughts

I used to question my thoughts by asking: "Is this true?"

Is it true that I'm not worthy? That I'm not good enough? That I'm not lovable?

I'd then look for evidence to prove that what I was believing wasn't, in fact, true. And when I found more empowering evidence, I'd feel better. But then the thoughts would revisit and I'd forget the empowering evidence, and I'd be back to square one. The whole process of inquiry would ultimately exhaust me.

Eventually, I realized that I didn't actually care if a thought was true or not. I cared more about whether or not it was useful.

Is it useful for me to believe that I'm not worthy? (Duh, no.)

Is it helpful for me to think I'm not good enough? (Definitely not.)

Am I doing myself a service by believing I'm not lovable? (Never.)

So now, when a challenging thought is present and persistent, I'll pause and ask: Is this useful?

If it's useful and offers constructive input, I'll journal to hear it out. And if it's not, I'll acknowledge its presence and let it know: "I'm good, thank you."

(TRY THIS

Write out a list of your current challenging thoughts. For each one, ask: Is this useful? If not, thank it and let it go. If it is, get curious: How can I listen in and learn from it?

Worry Better

Research shows that 85 percent of the things we worry about never actually happen. Think about it: How often do you say, "I'm so glad I worried about that for so long?" Maybe never?

When you feel yourself falling into a trap of what I call "toxic worry" (the ruminating and spinning thoughts that tend to paralyze you), pause, take a few deep breaths, and ask yourself two questions:

I'M SO GLAD I WORRIED ABOUT THAT FOR SO LONG ↰↲

said no one ever

> 1. Is this thought helping me or hindering me?
> 2. Is there any productive action I can take?

If it's useful and you can take productive action, make note of the best next thing you can do—and then go do that thing.

If it's not useful, and there isn't productive action for you to take, thank the thought for visiting and trying to keep you safe. (Because ultimately that's what worry is trying to do: protect you.) Then, remind the worry, "I can handle this," and imagine the thought floating away.

Over time, you'll learn that the more you can treat your worries with kindness and compassion, the worries won't act out or stir up more drama. You can train your mind to worry more effectively and you can determine what's actually worth investing energy in.

What is an ongoing worry you have? Is the thought helping or hindering you? Is there any productive action you can take to transform the worry into wonder?

Create Safety from Within

During rough seas, you can train yourself to create calm and safety from within, and that will inspire calm in others.

One place to begin is with the inner child that lives within you. Just like any child, your inner child may need help meeting their needs. When we turn toward our inner child with a compassionate ear, we can help them to feel safe, seen, and heard.

TRY THIS

Pull out a journal, and at the top of the page write:

Dear inner child, it's me. I'm here to listen. What do you need to feel safe right now?

Then, free-flow write, as if your inner child is speaking to you, until that part of you feels seen.

Once you feel complete in answering that question, ask your inner child: When you start to feel anxious, overwhelmed, or afraid, what do you need from me?

Then, free-flow write once again, until your inner child expresses what they need.

No matter what's happening in the world outside of you, these questions will help you create stillness and safety from within, which will inspire calm in others.

TRUST IN THE NONLINEAR SOUL PATH

Trust the Nonlinear Path

A few years ago, I thought I wanted to be a muralist. In my mind, the idea of channeling emotions into art seemed so romantic. But then I painted a few paintings and created a mural, and I pretty much hated the actual work of it.

I share this story as a reminder that it can be easy to lock yourself into projects and career paths because you like the *idea* of them, but when you get into the process of actually doing the work, it feels far less inspired and aligned.

While you don't need to love every second of what you create, when it comes to your life's work, the curiosity and desire ought to outweigh the dread.

Think about it: What's on your plate right now? Is there anything you've been holding on to, but you feel like it's time to shift?

Sometimes projects want us to pivot our role in them or outsource what's draining. Other times we may discover that we've been forcing ourselves into projects that we've outgrown, and it's time to let go.

Above all, remember: it's okay to shift course. When you approach life as an experiment, the entire point is to try ideas on, see how they feel and fit, do more of what works, and let go of the rest. Trust in the nonlinear soul path.

Remove yourself from it

Change it

or

Embrace it fully

Make a Choice

When a situation in your life is creating stress, there are three options:

1. Take yourself out of the situation.

2. Change it.

3. Accept and embrace it fully.

That's it. That's all we can ever do.

Which will you choose?

PUSH

PULL

PUSH	PULL
Feels like pushing a rock up a mountain	Feels like being pulled by a higher vision
Effort, effort	Align, align
Outcome-focused	Journey-oriented
I need to make this happen	I make things so things happen

Cultivate the Pull

We live in a "push" culture. It's outcome-driven, future-focused, and the narrative is: exerting effort is the only way to make things happen.

The challenge is that it can easily leave you feeling exhausted, out of touch with yourself, and, at worst, sick. The antidote I've found to push is pull.

When Push says, "This is the outcome I want, and I won't stop until I get there," Pull says, "This is the vision I'm wholeheartedly committed to and pulled toward. I trust where I'm being led."

When Push is always inclined to jump to "What's next?" Pull is intent on "What's now?"

Push believes things won't happen unless we do them; Pull believes doing what brings us joy can be a gravitational pull for outcomes that we'd never be able to imagine or predict.

Where do you stand on the push-and-pull spectrum? How might you invite more pull into your life today?

Create Clear Priorities

Whenever I notice myself saying, "I don't have enough time to do that," or "I'm so busy," I realize what I'm actually saying is "I don't know what's important right now."

When you feel overwhelmed, one of the best things you can do is pause and reflect on what's most important at this moment.

I don't have ~~enough~~ ~~time~~ clear priorities

I tend to find that my anxiety and angst has less to do with how many things I want to get done, and more about whether or not I'm spending my time and energy on the most important one or two things each day. So long as I'm creating space for what's most meaningful—I tend to feel better about what I do (and don't) get done.

Here are some questions to help you clarify your priorities (feel free to choose one or answer them all—whatever feels best):

1. What is my number-one priority right now?

2. Is there anything I'm saying "yes" to right now when I really want to say "no" or "not right now"? Why? What can I do to take this off my plate temporarily or permanently?

3. Is there anything I'm saying "yes" to that I *do* want, but it isn't serving me or what's important right now? How can I delegate or reschedule these things to create more spaciousness and ease?

4. How much of my energy is directed toward things that feel like a burden or obligation? How can I make them feel like less of a burden, and/or how I can do them less?

5. In terms of where I'm investing my time right now, what brings me the most fulfillment and joy? How can I do more of those things?

As author Annie Dillard says, "How we spend our days is, of course, how we spend our lives."

Invest wisely.

THE ENERGY MATRIX

LIFE-GIVING

JOY
QUALITY TIME
SELF-EXPRESSION
PRESENCE
NATURE

DEVOTION
SHOWING UP
FOLLOW THROUGH
SAYING "NO"
SPEAKING UP

I WANT TO

I HAVE TO*

* I GET TO (ON A GOOD DAY)

INDULGENCE
TOO MUCH "YES"
3RD GLASS OF WINE
MORE SCROLLING
DRAMA

OBLIGATION
TAXES
LEGAL TO-DOS
SOME FAMILY STUFF ☺
UNSPOKEN AGREEMENTS

LIFE-SUCKING

Explore the Energy Matrix

You will find no shortage of books, articles, podcasts, and videos about time management. But we talk far less about something more important: energy management.

When you think about all of the relationships, roles, projects, and experiences in your life, how much energy do they give you?

I created this energy matrix to help you learn more about what is giving and taking away from your personal energy.

On one axis, you've got the things you *want* to do on one side, and the things you *have* to do (or on a good day, *get* to do) on the other side. On the other axis, you have things that are life-*giving* and things that are life-*sucking*.

Just about everything that takes up space in your life falls into one of these four areas.

It's become a popular question these days to ask yourself: Does this bring me joy? While I love this question, I also find having a more full picture helps.

There is a time, place, space, and sometimes even necessity for not only things that bring you joy, but also things that are more of a "have to" and less of a "want to."

When thinking about how you manage your time, think about your energy too.

Your energy levels will thank you for it.

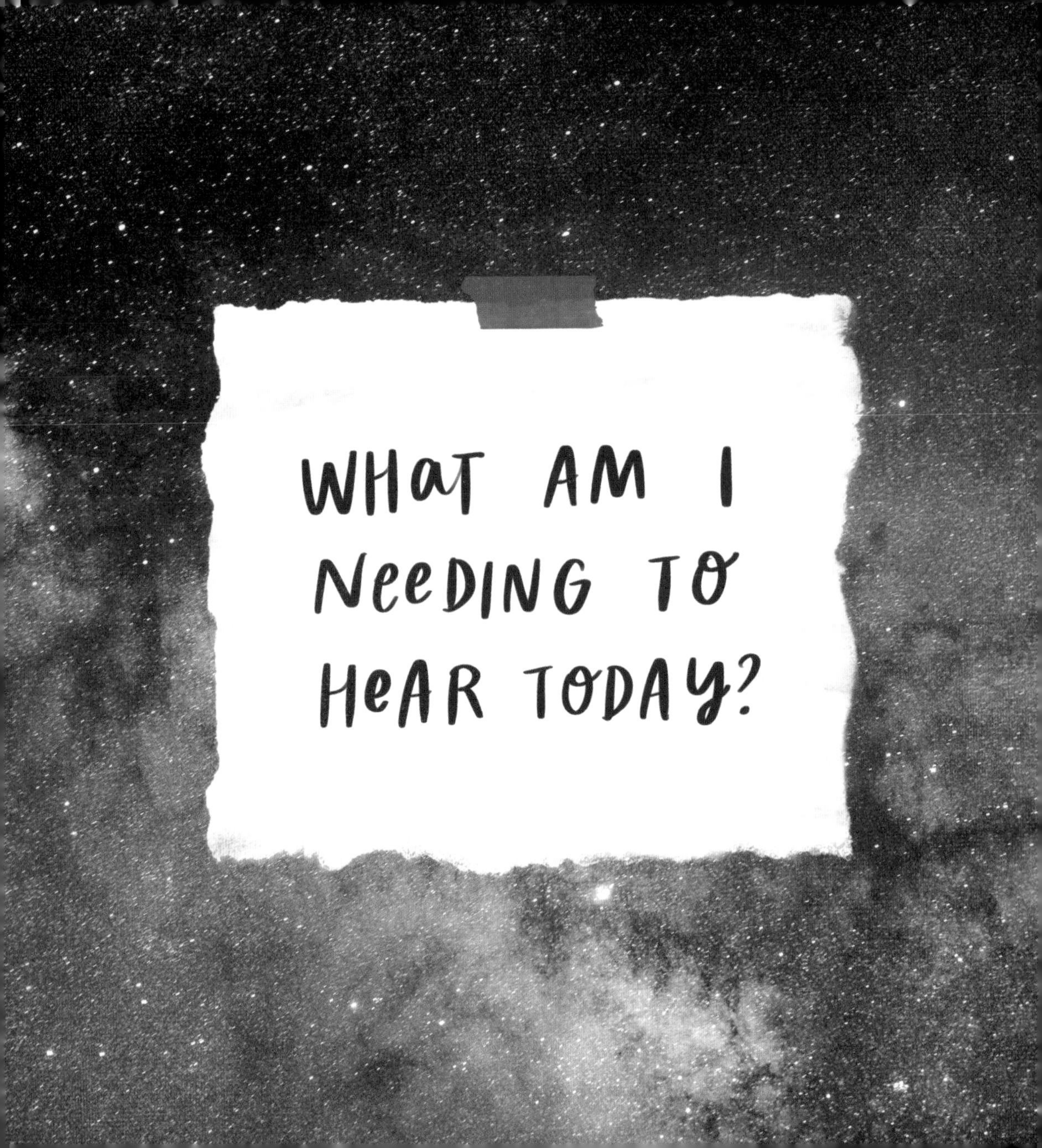
WHAT AM I NEEDING TO HEAR TODAY?

Be What You Need

Whenever I'm inclined to look outside of myself for reassurance or answers, I find it helpful to pause and instead ask myself:

What am I needing to hear right now?

Maybe I'm looking for permission to rest and disconnect without feeling guilty. Perhaps I'm wanting to be reminded that I'm exactly where I need to be. Or maybe I'm seeking reassurance that it's okay to feel exactly the way that I am.

When we ask ourselves what we need to hear, we become present to our own longings and inner world—so we can tend to our own needs and source wisdom from within.

Look inward, love. What are you needing to hear right now?

Show Up or Shut Down

Show Up or Shut Down

Researcher Brené Brown describes vulnerability as "uncertainty, risk, and emotional exposure." It's that shaky feeling we get when we step out of our comfort zone or do something that forces us to relinquish control. "Vulnerability is not weakness," Brené says; "it's our greatest measure of courage."

That shaky feeling may be present during a huge life event, like deciding to make a leap in your career; or it may be in the small moments, like telling a friend how their actions hurt you; asking for forgiveness when you've made a mistake; or setting a boundary with a family member.

While speaking up and expressing yourself may feel uncomfortable, you're also opening yourself up to growth, depth, and connection—all while honoring what's true for you.

So when shaky feelings arise, remember: it's natural when you're stepping outside of your comfort zone. And in response to these very natural feelings, you have two choices:

1. Show up: lean in to the discomfort and see it as an opportunity to learn, grow, and be courageous.

2. Shut down: hide from and avoid the discomfort. Run away.

What's causing you to feel vulnerable lately? How might you show up rather than shut down?

HOW IT FEELS TO HAVE A HARD CONVO

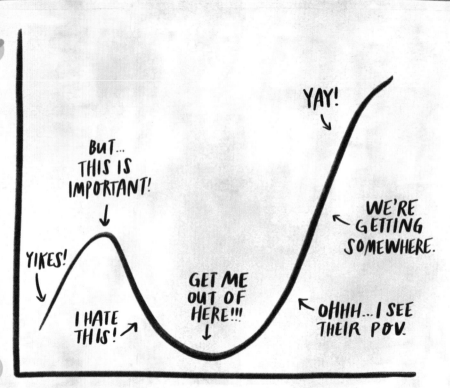

Have Hard Conversations

Hard convos are, well, hard. But the hardest part isn't the very beginning of the conversation—it's the middle. In the beginning, we know it's important and we feel hopeful for clarity and resolution. But when we get to the middle? That's when we may be inclined to shut down or run away.

When having a hard conversation, what's important is to *stay* through the discomfort.

Consider holding the intention—as hard as it may be—to listen and understand rather than speak and be understood. This will give you room to see things from another perspective and, in turn, put the other person at ease so they also have the emotional space to listen to and understand you.

It's a journey of a lifetime to learn how, in the heat of difficult conversations, to take responsibility when there's something for us to own, and to speak very honestly about what isn't working and what we need.

Honest convos, while hard, open the doorway to greater intimacy and trust. That is, if we stay through them.

BLAMING LANGUAGE → RESPONSIBLE LANGUAGE

Blaming Language	Responsible Language
You make me angry	I feel angry right now
They expect too much	My boundaries could be more clear
I can't do that	I'm choosing not to
It's your fault	I contributed to this

Stop the Blame Game

It is all too common that, when something goes wrong in our important relationships, the default is often to look for something or someone to blame, instead of taking responsibility.

When in "blame" mode, we say things like, "You made me feel this way," or "It's your fault," or "They won't let me."

Blame mode is a form of protection, because we guard ourselves from feeling disappointment, sadness, or regret—and it helps us feel a sense of control over the situation. While blaming others might provide temporary relief, we miss opportunities for empathy and emotional connection.

The next time you catch yourself pointing blame at someone you care for, take a moment to pause and point the finger back at yourself. What are you feeling? What do you need? How have you contributed to this conflict? Try to see it as an opportunity to accept responsibility, even if only partially. When we hold ourselves accountable in our close relationships, it paves the way to intimacy, meaning, and growth.

How to Have Hard Convos

ACKNOWLEDGE THE OTHER PERSON

I felt seen when you...

or

You were there for me when...

RELEASE JUDGMENT & PRACTICE COMPASSION

I don't understand why you can't... → Help me understand why you...

OWN THE STORY YOU'VE CREATED

the story I'm creating is...

OR

when X happened, I made it mean...

REFLECT BACK WHAT YOU HEAR

What I'm hearing you say is... ______

Am I hearing that right?

SPEAK FROM FIRST PERSON

you're not... → I need...

you're making me feel... → I feel...

HOW TO FILTER FEEDBACK

How much of this is useful or about me?

How much of this is about the other person?

What steps can I take to re-center or speak my truth?

Filter Feedback Wisely

Feedback can help us grow and see our blind spots, but not all feedback is created equal. It depends on whom it's coming from and what's motivating them to share.

Sometimes people offer feedback because they have a sliver of wisdom that can relate to our situation. Other times, their own fearful stories cloud them from seeing us as we are.

When the latter happens, and especially when that feedback is unsolicited, it can be natural to take it personally or make their behavior mean we are doing something wrong.

What's important to remember is that how people show up is a reflection of their own reality and worldview. Sometimes their "feedback" has nothing to do with us, and everything to do with their own stuff.

Either way, receiving feedback is a good practice in discerning what's useful and knowing when to create energetic boundaries.

Here are a few questions to ask yourself when filtering feedback:

1. Does this person have lived experience that connects to my situation?

2. Do I get the sense that this feedback is about truly supporting me?

3. What, if anything, can I take and learn from? What can I let go of?

Filter wisely.

Climb the Pyramid of Transformation

When we hold on to painful experiences from our past, it can create a cage around our hearts. We can become trapped in a story about who we need someone to be rather than accepting who they are.

When we find ourselves in a disempowering relationship dynamic—which sounds like "It's their fault," or "They did this to me"—it is an indicator that we are stuck in a pattern of shame and blame. If the relationship is important to you and you want to break free of the past, here are five stages to walk through:

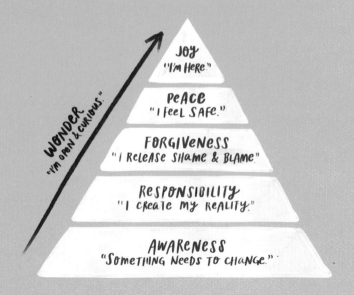

WONDER
"I'm open & curious."

JOY
"I'm Here."

PEACE
"I feel Safe."

FORGIVENESS
"I Release Shame & Blame."

RESPONSIBILITY
"I Create My Reality."

AWARENESS
"Something Needs to Change."

Awareness: "I realize something isn't working and needs to change."

Responsibility: "I recognize that I create my reality. While I cannot change the past, I am responsible for and committed to my healing and growth today. I am actively scripting the narrative I choose to lead my life moving forward."

Forgiveness: "I release shame and blame. I realize that holding on hurts me more than others. I recognize that they were doing the best they could. I let go of what could have been different and choose acceptance. I am more committed to my joy than my pain."

Peace: "I no longer hold an emotional charge about the event. I now see how the experience strengthened me and helped me grow. I feel gratitude for my revelations and heightened awareness. I feel love and compassion toward others and me. I feel safe and at home within myself. I feel free."

Joy: "I am here, in this moment, fully. I am present to what is today."

Is there a relationship in your life that you're looking for more peace and joy in? What stage of the pyramid are you in? What do you need to move into the next stage?

~~Forgiveness~~
~~means what they~~
~~did is okay~~

Forgiveness
sets me free

Let Forgiveness Set You Free

When we withhold forgiveness and hold on to anger, resentment, and blame, we suffer because we keep the feelings of hurt and pain alive.

Forgiveness sets you free because you give yourself the gift of peace. This doesn't mean you condone the others' actions or that their behavior was okay. Forgiveness releases you from the pain—so you can heal and move forward in your life.

GET CURIOUS

Who have you been hesitating to forgive? Why?
How might you benefit from letting go?

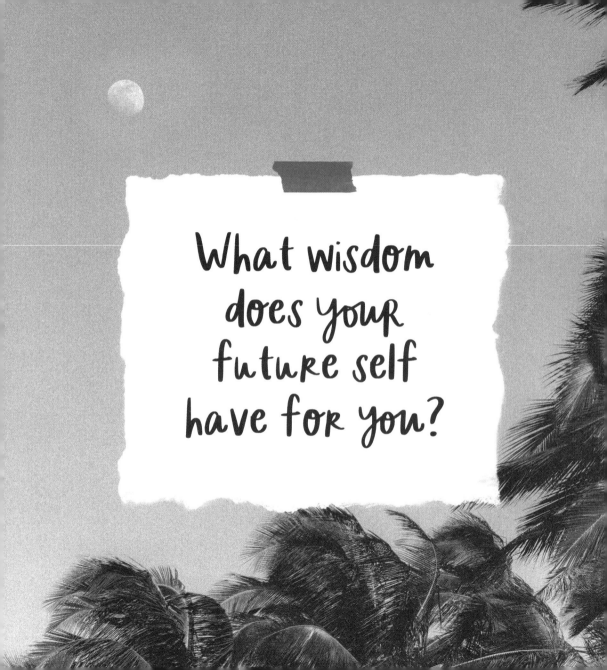

Your Future Self Is Wise

One day, your future self will look back on this period in your life with a perspective that might be hard to see right now.

What if you could tap into a sliver of that wisdom today?

I believe you have the wisdom of many lifetimes within you. Sometimes it's hard to listen when the noise of your inner critic and the world around you gets in the way. To tap into that wise inner knowing, here is a practice to try on:

TRY THIS

Write a letter from your wise future self to your present self.

To begin, pull out your journal and write at the top:

Hey [your name], *it's me, your wise future old self. Here's what I want you to know. . . .*

Ask your future self for perspective on a current challenge or burning question. Set a timer for ten minutes and write without pausing. You'll be surprised by what pours out of you—a stream of wisdom, ready to be tapped whenever you create space to listen.

WHOLENESS FEELS LIKE

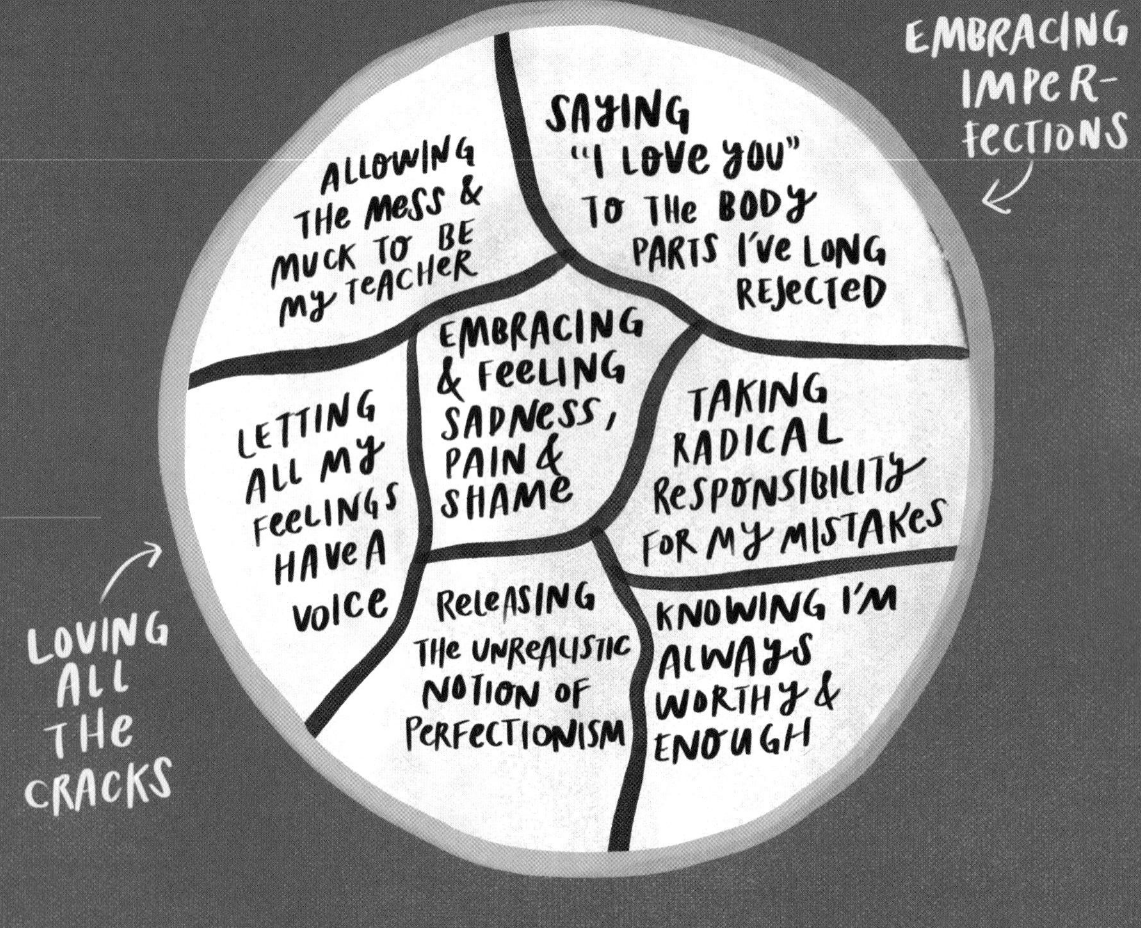

The Beauty in What's Broken

When I think about the journey of healing through painful times, I think about a concept called Kintsugi.

Kintsugi is the Japanese art of using gold lacquer to glue broken pottery back together. The process doesn't hide the cracks or the fact that the pottery shattered; it celebrates how those cracks make the art even more unique. The breakage and repair become part of the history of the object, rather than something to disguise it.

I love this as a metaphor for life.

When we go through challenging times, we may crack and shatter and fall apart. But when we tend to our broken parts and piece them back together with love, care, and compassion, we learn to celebrate our imperfections and find peace with our cracks.

So the next time it feels like life is breaking apart, remember that your cracks make you who you are, and only you hold the golden glue.

NOT TAKING RESPONSIBILITY
They are not respecting me
TAKING RESPONSIBILITY
I'm not setting clear boundaries

Own Your Part

I recently noticed a thought I was experiencing on repeat: "They're not respecting me. They're asking too much of me. Why are they doing this to me?" When I spotted the story-on-repeat, I smiled as I realized I was slipping into a disempowering mindset.

Generally, when I point the blame at someone else and think they are doing something "to me," it's an opportunity to pause, and turn the thought around to a statement that begins with "I." That's owning my part.

Here are a few examples:

1. "They are not respecting me" becomes "I am not setting or expressing clear boundaries."

2. "They don't appreciate me" becomes "I appreciate me for [X, Y, Z]."

3. "Why is this happening to me?" becomes "I'm contributing to this situation by . . ."

4. "They won't let me" becomes "I'm not letting myself because . . ."

When we frame a situation through the lens of responsibility, we reclaim our power and pave a path of integrity and action.

Is there a situation or relationship currently in your life for which it would feel empowering to own your part?

HOW TO SET BOUNDARIES

I VALUE	SO I NEED	& WILL HONOR BY
MY WELL-BEING	TO SAY "NO" WHEN IT'S NOT A TRUE "YES"	STAYING TRUE WHEN THERE IS EXTERNAL PRESSURE
ENERGY & CLARITY	PERSONAL TIME	HAVING A FIRM MORNING RITUAL
GROWTH	TO TEST MY LIMITS	TAKING ACTION WHEN I'M AFRAID
HONESTY	TO BE REAL WITH MYSELF AND OTHERS	ADDRESSING & ADJUSTING

Set Heart-Centered Boundaries

Clear boundaries can be the greatest contributors to our joy, freedom, and self-respect.

When you set a heart-centered boundary, you are drawing a line around how you honor and stay true to yourself, which is how people learn to treat you.

For example, if you continually say "yes" when you really mean "no," it's likely because you're valuing harmony and approval over self-worth and inner truth. People may then learn to rely on you to put their needs above your own, which is on you to shift.

Setting boundaries begins by knowing what they are. Here are three prompts to get started:

1. Values: What do I value? What is a nonnegotiable in my life?

2. Needs: What do I need to experience that value?

3. Actions to honor me: What does it look like to honor that need? What happens if it's not met?

What do you value, and how will you honor it? Use this framework to get clear on your dearest values, needs, and self-honoring actions.

THE SWEET SPOT

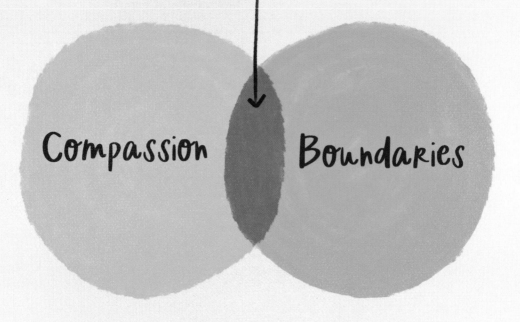

Compassion

Boundaries

Find Your Boundaries' Sweet Spot

My mom jokes that my favorite word is "no" and that boundaries are my best friend. As a former people pleaser, this feels like quite the accomplishment.

Here are a few things I've learned in my boundary-setting journey:

1. Boundaries aren't mean, selfish, or unkind. They show self-respect. They indicate what is and is not okay for your life.

2. We can't expect people to read our minds or know our boundaries. It's our responsibility to voice our needs, and we can do so with compassion and care— unless the situation calls for us to be firm and fierce.

3. Not everyone will respond well when we set boundaries, and we're not responsible for their reactions. We are, however, responsible for our delivery and how we respond to their reactions.

4. When creating or communicating a boundary, connect it to a core value. (E.g., you might say: "Because I value rest, I don't work on weekends." Or: "Because we value safety, here are the rules for this community. . . .")

5. Anger can be an ally in recognizing your boundaries. It shows you what you are and are not willing to tolerate.

As Brené Brown says, "Compassionate people ask for what they need. They say 'no' when they need to, and when they say 'yes,' they mean it. They're compassionate because their boundaries keep them out of resentment."

So. Much. *Yes.*

HOW TO KNOW YOUR BOUNDARIES

NEGOTIABLE

NON-NEGOTIABLE

Hard lines to live your values

soft guidelines & preferences

- HONESTY
- VITALITY
- QUALITY TIME
- PERSONAL RESPONSIBILITY
- PLAY & REST

- SLEEP SCHEDULE
- HEALTH PRACTICES
- HOME BASE

Create Your Boundary Ring

Knowing your boundaries is having awareness around what is and is *not* okay for you. Setting boundaries is having the courage to love yourself and respect your values, even at the risk of disappointing others.

Let's talk about the difference between negotiable and *non*negotiable boundaries. Negotiable boundaries are soft guidelines that are open for discussion. These preferences won't have you leave a situation or relationship for your well-being, but they are points around which to have honest conversations and create agreements.

Nonnegotiable boundaries, on the other hand, are what you need to feel safe and secure in your life. They are *not* open for discussion or change because negotiating on them in any way would force you to betray yourself or live outside your core values. This applies to romantic partners, family members, friends, colleagues, work environments, your body, and at home.

Use this graph as a tool to clarify your negotiables and nonnegotiables for the different areas of your life (e.g., love, sex, work, family, friendships, spirituality, creativity, money) so that you can protect and honor what matters most to you. Here are two questions to get started:

What boundaries are important to you, but flexible?

What boundaries are essential to your sense of being honored, respected, and secure?

I'm here for you.

Create a Safe Space

When someone we love is facing a hardship, or we ourselves are experiencing difficulty, we have an opportunity to create a space of safety rather than shame. It starts with the words we use.

Instead of "Don't be upset," we can say instead, "I hear that you're feeling upset. Thank you for letting me in."

Instead of "Don't cry," we can say instead, "It's okay to feel upset. It's okay to cry. I'm here."

Instead of "Don't be so sensitive," we can say instead, "I see that this is impacting you deeply."

Instead of "Don't overthink it," we can say instead, "I can see how much you care about this."

Simple tweaks in language create safety, belonging, and connection. When in doubt, these four words—"I'm here for you"—can make a world of a difference.

WHAT TO DO WHEN YOU MESS UP

We all make mistakes we regret, say things we don't mean, and act in ways that are out of alignment with our values. What matters is how we respond when we mess up. Here are a few tips for when you mess up:

Forgive yourself

Shaming yourself won't help you heal or move forward. Making mistakes doesn't make you a bad person. You're human. You're learning. Embrace your evolving journey.

Reflect on what happened & what you learned

Take a step back to get perspective by asking yourself: Why did this happen? How did I get myself in this situation? What did I learn here?

Take responsibility & apologize

Own your mess-up. Acknowledge where you fell short and the impact it had on those involved. When you can't change what happened, be proactive about repairing the situation.

Commit to change

Failures help us learn and grow—so long as we take the time to reflect on what the situation is teaching us. Once you feel clear on the lessons, consider what you'll do and how you'll respond should you find yourself in a similar situation in the future. When we imagine it in advance, we're more likely to live into it.

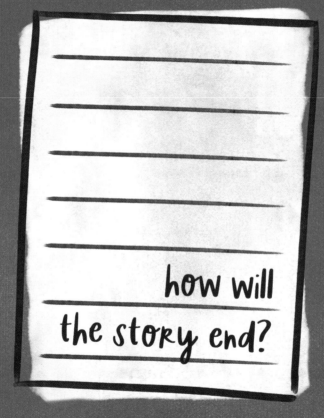

Write a Brave Ending

An ex-boyfriend reached out once and said, "Hey, I'm sorry for how I hurt you and the ways I didn't show up to our relationship. I shut down and pushed you away because I didn't know any better. I just want you to know that I'm so grateful for the time we shared together."

I was floored. I felt seen and heard in a way that I didn't know I needed.

And it got me wondering . . .

Is there someone in my life who would benefit from me acknowledging how I fell short in our relationship? What could I say to have them feel seen?

I reached out to an old friend and an ex-boyfriend, acknowledging a time when I didn't show up as I would have liked and what I would have done differently if I could have a "redo." With each communication, I felt a sense of completion, integrity, and release. And while I couldn't control how they received or responded to me—I was, as always, in control of how the story ends.

How about you? Is there someone you've been meaning to reach out to? Is there a situation you regret, one that you'd like to own up to?

Remember: you get to choose how your story ends.

Create your own closure

Create Your Own Closure

It can be difficult to move forward when we don't get the closure we'd like.

Maybe a relationship ends painfully and without clear resolution. An animal we love goes missing out of the blue. Or we face conflict with someone who's not willing to make amends.

All of these experiences can leave us wondering, waiting, and hoping for more. It can send us spiraling into hurt feelings and painful memories—longing for closure without knowing how to close the door.

How do we find peace so we can move on? How do we accept the past so we can live more fully in the present?

What I've discovered is this: healing comes through finding closure within myself instead of looking to others to give it to me.

A practice that's helped is writing a letter to the person I'm seeking closure with. Because I don't send it, it's a way to get all of my thoughts and feelings out on paper—so that I can process, grieve, forgive, and let go.

Here's how it works: in the letter, write down why they hurt you, what you wanted them to say or do that they didn't, what you wish you could have said or done differently, and what you forgive them and yourself for. When you're finished, say "Thank you and goodbye."

If you're feeling bold, burn the letter to mark a new beginning.

swim in gratitude

swim in gratitude

swim in gratitude

Swim in Gratitude

Sometimes it takes something being taken away from us in order to realize how much we appreciate it.

When loss or change occur, activities and people we may have otherwise taken for granted quickly become rare and precious pleasures. One of the side effects of experiencing hardship is that, suddenly, you can see all of the things you have to be grateful for in Technicolor.

Today, I invite you to cultivate the practice of gratitude in spite of (or because of) any recent hardships. Here are some questions to reflect on:

What are three things that happened recently that you're grateful for? Why?

What have you taken for granted that you're especially grateful for now?

What have others done for you lately that you're grateful for? (Bonus: go thank them!)

LISTEN

GUIDE

OR

SOLVE

Listen, Guide, or Solve?

Whenever someone I love is confiding in me about a challenging situation and I notice myself wondering how I can help (and especially when I'm feeling a bit helpless not knowing *how* I can help), I find it useful to ask:

Do you want me to listen, guide you through this, or help you solve it?

I let them tell me what they need—and I show up accordingly.

THIS IS HOW you SHOULD FIX IT...

Support Me, Don't Save Me

When we try to "fix" other people's problems, it can be a strategy for avoiding our own uncomfortable emotions. Rather than sit with and accept that we feel unsettled about the challenges the people we care about face, we may be inclined to fix it for them.

I get it. It's heartbreaking to see the people we love struggle. But the downfall of the savior strategy? We're not giving them the opportunity to locate courage and solve it on their own.

The distinction between fixing other people's problems and supporting them to solve their own is an important one.

WHAT DO you NEED RIGHT NOW?

Fixing means avoiding your own feelings, helping to feel needed, giving unsolicited advice, feeling resentful when they don't listen, and enabling unhealthy behaviors. We may think our desire to help comes from love, but often it's fear in disguise.

Supporting is compassion in action. It means showing up, offering a listening ear, asking questions to help the person make their own informed decisions, giving advice when it's solicited, and seeing others as capable of solving their own stuff.

GET CURIOUS

Can you think of a recent situation when you tried to "fix" a challenge for someone? How might you support the person to solve it instead?

Reset Your Habits

How do we shift habits that are difficult to change?

The most important realization I've had is this: everything I do is to feel a certain way. When I can unpack why I'm doing something and the benefit it gives me (such as stress release or pleasure), I can replace it with something I enjoy and value just as much—and oftentimes, so much more.

Let's take the habit of grabbing my phone when I wake up as an example. I know that scrolling through social media and checking my email is not how I want to start my day. But can you guess the benefit it gives me? It kicks me into alertness and literally wakes me up. But with it also comes stress, anxiety, and a sense of overwhelm first thing in the morning. Knowing that I want to tune in with myself before I greet the day, I now place my phone in another room and have replaced it with a sacred ritual: each morning I ask myself the question, "What will create aliveness and nourishment for me right now?" and then I honor myself by doing that thing.

Is there a habit you've been holding on to that you'd like to reset? Here are five steps to shift hard-to-break habits:

1. Clarify the habit you want to change. What's no longer serving you? What have you outgrown?

2. Unpack what it gives you. What benefit do you get from this habit? How does it make you feel?

3. Find a replacement. What do you value more? What will help you feel how you *really* want to feel?

4. Commit to a tiny step. What small step can you realistically commit to starting today?

5. Create accountability. Who can support you in staying true to your goal?

HOW TO ReSeT HABITS

HABIT I WANT TO CHANGE:	WHAT IT GIVES ME:	WHAT I CAN REPLACE IT WITH:	SO... I WILL:
WAKE UP & GRAB PHONE	ENERGY & CONNECTION	STRETCHING & JOURNALING	MOVE PHONE TO OTHER ROOM
CRITICAL SELF-TALK	A SENSE OF CONTROL	HUMOR & DETACHMENT	NICKNAME MY CRITIC
SITTING ALL DAY	PRODUCTIVITY & FLOW	WALKING MEETINGS	SCHEDULE AS SUCH
EVENING WINE	PLEASURE & RELAXATION	EVENING STROLL	WALK TONIGHT

What's one choice you will make today that your future self will thank you for?

Make Feel-Good Choices

When I'm struggling to feel empowered around a habit or action that's important to me, I find it helpful to think of my present and future selves as two separate people.

Maybe my present self doesn't want to grab my journal, do the fifteen-minute meditation, or sit with an uncomfortable emotion—but I know my future self is going to feel grounded and peaceful.

Maybe my present self really wants that extra glass of wine because it feels pleasurable in the moment—but I know my future self won't feel great in the morning.

Maybe my present self wants to stay within her comfort zone and not share her truths with the world—but I know my future self is eager to evolve and create.

In what way is your present self stifling you? What's one choice you can make today that your future self will thank you for?

you CAN FeeL
HEARTBROKEN
FOR THE WORLD

& JOYFUL FOR
your LIFE at
THE SAME TIME.

Hold Space for Dualities

Most everything in life is a paradox.

Your weaknesses double as your greatest strengths.

You can feel joy and pain, gratitude and desire, confidence and insecurity at the same time.

You can wish for things now and be grateful later that they never happened.

You can try to shield yourself from discomfort at all costs, only to realize everything you truly want is on the other side of your fear.

We live in a culture that tells us we need to choose, but the truth is: we don't.

Fully embracing the ever-present paradoxes of life is one of the most expansive and liberating choices you can make in your life.

The more you can hold space for the full spectrum of emotions and experiences, the more you can be present for and enjoy the beautiful, paradoxical truths of your ever-unfolding life.

What paradox have you been thinking about in a limiting way? How would it feel to not have to choose one side or the other?

PERMISSION SLIP

I will give myself what I need today.

Write Your Permission Slip

Let's talk about permission. Where does it come from, and who gives it to us? For much of our lives, we learn to look to others for permission. Teachers, authority figures, our friend group, society. But the permission that really matters is the kind that you give to *yourself*.

You don't need permission to write, speak your truth, or act on what calls at your heart. You don't need permission to rest or slow down or change your mind. You don't need permission to laugh or cry or feel the full range of your emotions. You don't need permission on how to live your one life.

Your life belongs to *you*. What would it look like to give yourself permission to live as fully and freely as you'd like?

Take a moment to tune in:

What do I want to give myself permission to do right now?

Maybe it's permission to rest—remembering that downtime is productive, too.

Maybe it's permission to take a leap—even though you don't know where you're headed.

Maybe it's permission to make a mess—because life is an imperfect journey filled with many steps and *mis*steps.

Maybe it's permission to be angry—because rage can illuminate the injustices that are meaningful.

What permission slip will you write yourself today?

ACTING TOUGH BEING STRONG

ACTING TOUGH	BEING STRONG
Saying "I'm fine" when beneath the surface, something is not okay	Acknowledging & owning what you're feeling— and why
You mask your insecurities and try to cover up your shortcomings	You acknowledge your shortcomings and admit mistakes
You keep your challenges to yourself because you don't want to burden anyone	You ask for help, realizing it takes courage and humility

Be Strong, Not Tough

The message that "emotions make you weak" is interwoven into our culture in many destructive ways. Of all the myths about emotions, the weakness myth is perhaps the most dangerous.

It leads to internalized stigma and shame. It shuts down healthy conversations. It gets in the way of intimacy and trust. It makes us believe that something is "wrong" with us if we experience and feel difficult emotions.

Let's talk about the difference between *acting* tough and *being* strong:

Toughness acts like everything is okay when it's not; strength owns how you feel.

Toughness acts out for protection; strength channels emotions constructively.

Toughness masks insecurities; strength owns your shortcomings.

Toughness never asks for help; strength reaches out when support is needed.

How has "acting tough" shown up in your life, and what would it look like for you to embody strength instead?

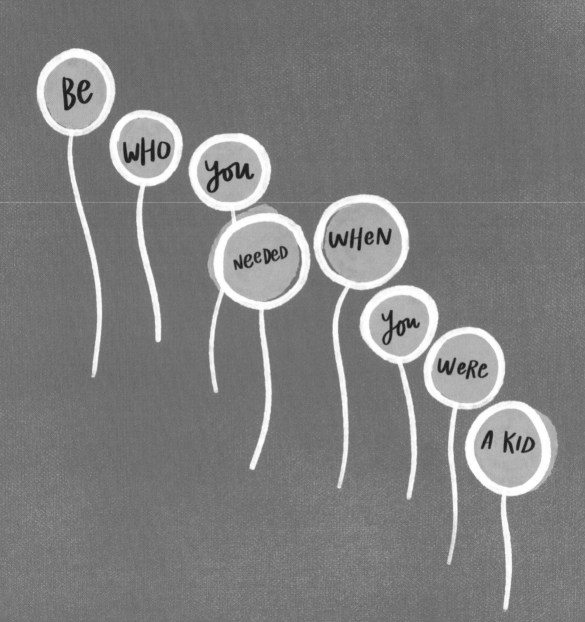

Be Who You Needed When You Were a Kid

Spend a few moments thinking about your memories as a kid. Trust whatever moment comes to mind first, then let them flow from there (it is amazing all of the things you'll remember that you haven't thought about in years!).

Now hone in on a moment in your younger life that felt transformative to you. It could be a moment that caused enormous pain or one that made you swell with joy—or somewhere in between.

What did you need from the world then?

Did you need encouragement? Someone to tell you they believed in you? Someone to say you are deeply loved? Could you have used compassion or comfort or a safe space?

As we grow up, we carry the needs of our inner children with us. The magic of holding on to these early needs and desires is that we become beautifully equipped at not only fulfilling them for ourselves—compassion, safety, self-love, encouragement, and so on—but also being what we used to need or want from others, *for* others.

If you craved encouragement as a kid, chances are you can more readily spot others who need encouragement around you now. If it was a physical safe space you really needed, no one knows better than you how to help others get there.

The person you needed when you were a kid? You can become—and in many ways probably already are—that person for yourself and for others.

What did the kid version of you need? How can you be that person today?

IF I LOVED
MYSELF FULLY,
HOW WOULD
I TREAT
MYSELF EACH
DAY?

Love Yourself Fully

It is true that the more we love ourselves, the better we treat ourselves. But it works the other way around, too.

The better we treat ourselves, the more we love ourselves.

If you don't fully feel like you love yourself or know your worth, one way to get there is by acting as if you already do.

CONSIDER:

If you loved yourself fully, how would you show up for yourself each day? What would your morning ritual look like? How would you nourish your body? How would you speak to yourself? What kinds of people would be in your life? What kinds of work would you do? What would standing in your worth look and feel like?

I invite you to ponder these questions today and notice when there may be room for more sacred self-care.

When we show up for ourselves, we remember who we are, we reclaim our power, and we model to others how we want to be treated.

What small thing will you do today to honor and love yourself?

You deserve to be loved.

The fear of feeling TOO GOOD

Let Yourself Feel Good

I've noticed an interesting pattern in myself and others when we begin taking steps in meaningful directions. Yes, there's the fear of failure, rejection, or not being good enough.

But what about the fear of feeling too good? *Too* much joy? *Too* much success? *Too* much bliss?

This happened recently when I moved out of New York and into nature. This transition was many years in the making, and when we arrived, my body took the deepest exhale. We were suddenly surrounded by palm trees and chirping birds and warm sunshine and the smell of ocean air. I squealed with glee.

Then the anxious thoughts started to spin: "You should feel guilty for getting to experience this," and "Are you sure you deserve this?" My inner joy dissolved as I wronged myself for feeling good.

This phenomenon is what psychologist Gay Hendricks calls "Upper Limiting." It's the idea that we all have a certain level of comfort with feeling good. When we start to feel *too* good, we reach our "Upper Limit," and we begin to manufacture painful thoughts or images to bring us back to where we're more comfortable: not feeling so good.

Sound familiar?

When this fear arises, I take three steps:

1. Notice it. When the worries start spinning because I feel *too* good, I simply notice it. Being aware of the pattern helps me shift it.

2. Call it out—with love. I'll say, "Oh, hey there, Worry. I see you getting nervous about how good we're feeling right now. It's safe to feel joy. Thanks for trying to protect me, but I'm good."

3. Explore the root. I'll ask: Where did I learn that it's not okay to feel good? What am I afraid to lose? When I can pinpoint the origin story, I can choose to buy into a new story:

That feeling good is our birthright.

Choose Wonder over Worry

The way we choose to look at situations impacts how we respond to them. When I'm feeling challenged or uncertain or afraid and I want to tap into my wiser, more wondrous self, here's a practice that helps me:

Bring to mind the dilemma, hardship, or question that's weighing heavily on your heart.

First, look at the situation through a lens of Worry. How would you respond to this situation from a place of fear, despair, and control? (Really let yourself go there, feel it, and how it would play out.)

Then, look at the situation through the lens of Wonder. How might you respond to this situation from a place of curiosity, openness, and trust? (Again, really let yourself feel into that and how it would play out.)

As you imagine your responses, pay close attention to when you feel tightness in your body and when you feel a sense of ease.

Did you notice any answers or possibilities emerge when you tried on the lens of Wonder? Which way of living and leading resembles the kind of person you are—and ache to be?

While worry is the default mode for many of us, you can choose wonder over worry at any given moment. Who knows, it just might change everything.

Synchronicity Highway

Get on Synchronicity Highway

Have you ever experienced a set of coincidences that took your breath away?

Maybe you think of an old friend and then, out of the blue, you run into them on the street. Maybe you write down the name of a dream collaborator, and days later that person is sitting next to you at a dinner party. Maybe you declare a dream, one that feels a *tad* out of reach, and then you meet a new friend with the know-how to help you make it happen.

When support and clues show up seemingly out of the blue, I think of these kinds of magical moments as "being on synchronicity highway." They are reminders that I'm on the right path—and are a nudge from the universe to keep going.

right this way

Here's the thing about cosmic clues, though: we must be open to them and we must trust when they show up in our paths—because they are passageways to our highest potential.

I don't believe it's a coincidence that right now you are reading these words. Consider that you turned to this page for a reason—and at this exact moment in time, you are meant to be reading this.

The invitation here is this: to be open to what signs and support are in store for you today, because whatever is most needed on your path is on its way to you. You have to believe it to see it.

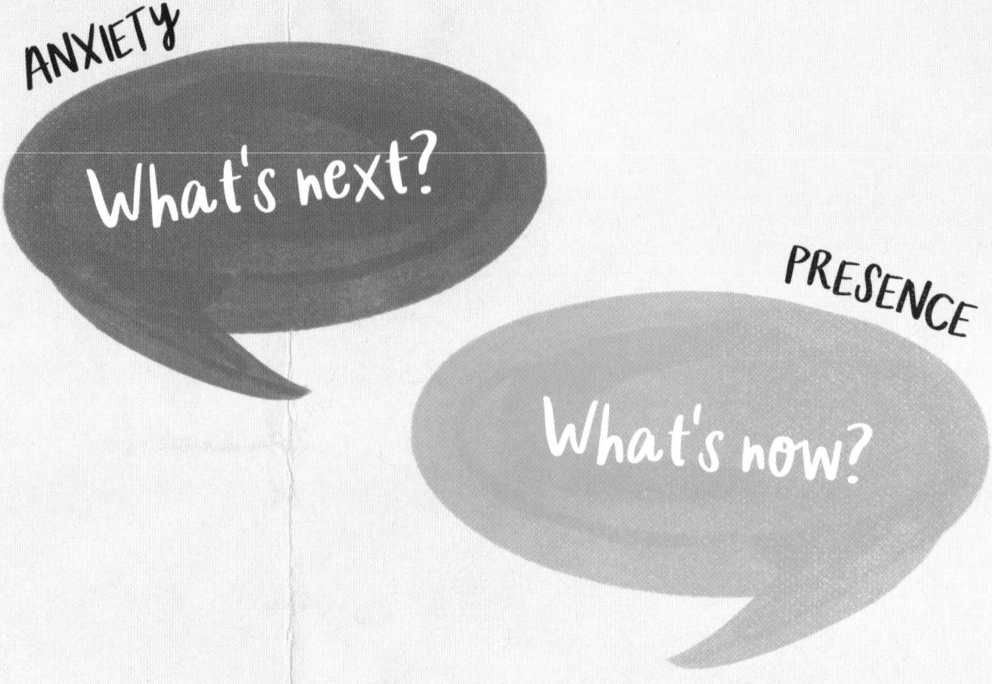
ANXIETY
What's next?
PRESENCE
What's now?

Focus on What's Now, Not What's Next

There are moments in our lives when it's important to be in a phase of asking: What's next?—when we're moving through our to-do list or making progress on an important project, for example.

When taken too far, the question What's next? may always have us trying to get somewhere else—filling the space in our lives with more and more—which can cause us to lose sight of the beauty that's already *here*.

When we ask ourselves what's here to appreciate right now, we become present to this moment and what *already* enriches our lives.

When you notice yourself striving, reaching, trying to get *there*—and all that effort is no longer serving you—remember to come back here, to this moment, and ask: What's already here for me to appreciate?

As spiritual teacher Ram Dass says, **"Be here now."**

Don't die with your gifts still inside

Don't Die with Your Gifts Still Inside

The untimely death of my father—a man I yearned to know as a child but never got the chance to really know, a man who ran from his demons rather than faced them, and a man who had so much to give but got in his own way—taught me one very important lesson:

Don't die with your gifts still inside.

Life is fragile; tomorrow isn't promised, and each day we are given a chance to do our best and share our gifts.

As Todd Henry shares in the book *Die Empty*, the most valuable land in the world is not Manhattan or the oil fields of the Middle East or the gold mines of South Africa. It's the graveyard. "In the graveyard are buried all the unwritten novels, never-launched businesses, unreconciled relationships, and all of the other things that people thought, 'I'll get around to that tomorrow.' One day, however, their tomorrows ran out."

Is there something you too have yearned to do—but you've been putting it off to *someday*?

Consider this a friendly reminder—and an invitation—to let someday start today.

Stay True to you

Stay True to You

After speaking at a women's conference about courageously expressing our gifts and "not dying with our gifts still inside," a woman approached me, crying.

"But I don't know what my gift is. . . ."

"You are the gift," I said. "Staying true to yourself is the greatest gift you can give to yourself and the world."

Stay true to you—in a world that tells you who to be and how to live.

Stay true to you—after the moments when you walk away from your inner knowing.

Stay true to you—because the path you're on is so much bigger and more beautiful than you can see right now.

Stay true to you—knowing you are in this exact moment on your path for a reason.

There's no need to search for your gift outside of you: it has and will always live within.

The world needs your story, your journey, your curiosities, your wisdom, your unique perspective.

Expressing and sharing those things as truthfully as possible in the world . . .

That is your gift.

Acknowledgments

I would first like to thank and acknowledge my community, who supported, shared, and validated this body of work. Without your thoughtful questions and inspired comments, this book would not exist. You mean the world to me and I made this book with my whole heart *for you*.

To my incredible agent, Sarah Passick, for seeing me, believing in my dreams, and helping me stay sane along the way. I treasure you.

To my editor and fairy godfather, Joel Fotinos, you remind me daily of the power of synchronicity and noticing life's clues. I am so blessed that our paths collided and I get to be guided by you.

To my design partner-in-crime, Maddie Nieman, for teaching me the magic of creative collaboration. It is no coincidence that we stumbled into each other's lives when we did. Working with you is a *dream* and I am eternally grateful.

To Melissa Joy Kong: I am awed by your heart, your devotion, and how you helped me bring this book into being. You are truly a *joy*.

To momma bear Beverly, for always encouraging me to live my truth, follow what calls me, and dream the biggest dream. I am who I am because of your love, support, and encouragement.

To Gwen Hawkes and the entire St. Martin's Publishing Group team who helped make this book possible. Thank you, thank you, thank you.

A special thank-you to my inner-circle soul fam: John, Laura, Allie, Sara, Shannon, Farhad, Majo, Erin, Shiva, and Lupita. Your care, love, and wisdom mean so much to me.

And to all who've supported my work over the years, thank you for being part of my heart. I appreciate you so much.

xo Amber Rae

About the Author

Amber Rae (@heyamberrae) is an author, artist, and global voice for creativity, self-discovery, and emotional wellness. She turns highly relatable insights on the human experience into viral art, sold-out venues, and bestselling books that help people transform their lives. She's the author of *Choose Wonder over Worry: Move Beyond Fear and Doubt to Unlock Your Full Potential*, and her work has been featured in publications such as *The New York Times*, *New York* magazine, *SELF*, *Fortune*, *Forbes*, and *Entrepreneur*. Amber has collaborated with brands such as Kate Spade, Apple, and ABC, and she reaches more than nine million people per month online with her words and art.